甲賀流　虎の巻

**PAUL H. CROMPTON LTD.,**
**638 Fulham Road, London S.W.6**

Magnificent Samurai — *Abelard, M.*
Basic Karate Katas — *Kanazawa, H.*
Kanku Dai — *Kanazawa, H.*
Basic Karate Katas Vol. 2 — *Smith, J.*
Competition Karate — *Valera, D.*
Introduction to Kung fu — *Jakab, L.*
Praying Mantis Kung fu — *Un, H.B.*
Nunchaku Training Manual — *MacLaren & Thompson*
Haraigoshi — *favourite judo techniques*
Seoinage — *favourite judo techniques*
Bassai Dai — Shotokan karate kata — *Anderson, J.*
Pak Mei Kung fu — *Un, H.B.*
Karate Defence and Attack — *Enoeda & Chisholm*
Karate Annuals 1 & 2 combined in one
Aikido introduction to Tomiki style — *Clapton, M. J.*
Shotokan karate free fighting techniques — *Enoeda & Mack*
Special Competition Karate — *Donovan & Valera*
Zen Combat — *Gluck, J.*
Tong Long Stick — praying mantis — *Un, H.B.*
Basic Forms of Shotokan Karate — *Anderson, J.*
Secret Techniques Wing Chun Kung Fu vol. 1 — *Chao/Weakland*
Taekwondo — *Huan, B. S.*
Primordial Pugilism, Tai Chi Chuan — Dr. Tseng Ju Pai
Pak Mei Tiger Fork — *Ng, J.*
Police Arrest Techniques — *Finn, M.*
Chong Woo Kwan Wing Chun — *Cheng, J.*
Beginning Ju Jitsu — *Shortt and Hashimoto*
Tomiki Aikido vol. 1 — *Dr. Lee Ah Loi*
Full Contact Martial Arts — *Warrener, D.*
Techniques of the Tonfa — *MacLaren and Thompson*
Tomiki Aikido vol. 2 — *Dr. Lee Ah Loi*
Gung Lik Kune kung fu — *Un, H.B.*
Dynamic Baton Techniques — *Wiszniewski, L.*
Secret Techniques of Wing Chun vol. 2 — *Chao/Weakland*
Fighting Fit — *MacLaren and Thompson*
Moving Zen — *Nicol*
Shukokai Karate Kata — *Morris T.*
Introduction to Shaolin Kung fu — *Wong, K. K.*
Tai Chi Weapons — *Dr. Tseng Ju Pai*

# TIGER SCROLLS

## of the

# KOGA NINJA

Jay Sensei

Paul H. Crompton Ltd.
638 Fulham Road,
London, S.W.6.
England.

ISBN 0 901764 70 1

Production co-ordination by
MM PRODUCTIONS LTD
1 Brookside
Hertford

Printed in Finland by
GUMMERUS Oy
Jyväskylä

JAY SENSEI
'The English Samurai'
Head Instructor of 'Z E N J I  K E N G O'
Began training in the Martial Arts in 1973.
Studied in Japan 1978 - 1983 under the following Teachers.
　　INOUE Sensei (KOBUDO, Master)
　　HANAMURA Sensei (KENJUTSU, Master)
　　SAITO Sensei (BUDO, Master)
　　YAMUGUCHI Sensei (AIKIDO, 8th. Dan)
　　HISASAKA Sensei (KEMPO, 8th. Dan)
　　NOGUCHI Sensei (KENJUTSU, 7th. Dan)
　　SEKIYA Sensei (KENJUTSU, 6th. Dan)
and AIKAWA Sensei (KEMBU, 'Sword Dance')

## WARNING

"None of the techniques or methods described in this
book should be attempted by anyone, as in the hands of
an untrained person would result in serious injury or
even death to the user."

JAY SENSEI

## NINJA NO CHIGIRI (Ninja's Covenant)

I will vanish into the night; change my body to wood or stone; sink into the earth and walk through walls and locked doors. I will fly like a bird and become a fish and live under water. I will be killed many times, yet will not die; change my face and become invisible, able to walk among men without being seen.

### I AM NINJA

My Parents are the Heaven and the Earth.
My Home is My Body.
My Power is Loyalty.
My Magic is Training.
My Life and My Death is Breathing.
My Body is Control.
My Eyes are the Sun and the Moon.
My Ears are Sensitivity.
My Laws are Self-Protection.
My Strength is Adaptability.
My Ambition is taking every Opportunity with Fullness.
My Friend is My Mind.
My Enemy is Carelessness.
My Protection is Right Action.
My Weapons are Everything that Exists.
My Strategy is One Foot in front of the Other.

### MY WAY IS NINJUTSU

# CONTENTS

# 史
## SHI
## (HISTORY)

*Ninja:* The Japanese Secret Assassins were not men of fiction, but did in fact exist in Ancient Japan from the Sixth Century to the beginning of the seventeenth Century. For over a thousand years they were the unknown, faceless men, available for hire by anyone to fulfil five functions: spying; gathering information; carrying secret messages; infiltrating the enemy to cause confusion before and during a battle and finally Killing and Assassinations.

Men of Invisibility who stalked the night and were total in their loyalty to their groups.

The Golden Age of the *Ninjas* began with the end of the *Muromachi* Era in 1467, continued through the *Sengoku* Era up to the beginning of the *Edo* Era which began in 1600.

Their ability to travel great distances, conceal themselves in their surroundings, disappear and re-appear, utilising anything and everything around them as weapons, made them men to be feared. Unlike the other elite group of men at that time, the *Samurai*, who also underwent harsh training, submitted to an unbelievably severe discipline and who were governed by a strict code of conduct, the *Ninja's* mission was of utmost importance. It had to be completed by any means, fair or foul.

In the Oriental character, the characteristic known as *losing face* or humiliation as we know it, was unacceptable to the *Samurai*, who would kill himself first rather than be humiliated or disgraced. The *Ninja*, however, would crawl before the enemy, humiliate himself as a short term necessity for the sake of the long term result of completing a mission.

The Laws of the *Ninjas* forbade them to tell anyone that they were *Ninjas* or to use *Ninjutsu* for their own benefit or reward. Should they break these laws and reveal the Secrets of *Ninjutsu*, they would be killed by their own group.

Throughout history they were known by many names such as *Kamarai*, *Rappa*, *Suppa*, and *Onmitsu*. In the *Edo* Era they were known as *Shinobi* and practised *Ninjutsu*. Later they were called *Ninja* and practised *Nimpo*.

Knowledge of medicines, weather forecasting, herbs, poisons and methods of strengthening the body were originally developed and used by the Priests of India. This knowledge travelled to China and then in the sixth century came to the mainland of Japan. They were adopted by select groups of soldiers, who founded the system that became *Ninjutsu* or the Way of the *Ninja*. From a method of maintaining good health to survive the rigorous life of a Priest and for self-protection, the knowledge was adapted to create a group of men who were experts at warfare, espionage and death.

In the sixth century, the seas around Japan were infested by Chinese Pirates who when attacking other ships or raiding coastal towns, would always send a group of men before an attack or during an attack to cause confusion among the enemy. As it meant almost certain death to the men in these special groups, they had to be men of a unique character, trained and brought up to believe totally in what they were told, obey an order without question and be prepared to give up their lives, not to a cause or belief, but so that a mission could be completed. Only the Oriental character can produce such men, who knowing beforehand that they would die, yet are willing to perform certain acts.

A region in Southern Japan, known as *Mie* Prefecture, was the first place where these foreign methods of training and warfare were used to develop special groups of men. This development was undertaken by the people of *Iga*.

In 593 A.D., the great Japanese Ruler Prince *Shotoku* was said to have used special groups of men for carrying messages and for espionage work. When the capital of Japan was moved from *Nara* to *Kyoto* in 794, these groups were sent into the new capital to gather information and silence any objectors.

From this period up to the end of the *Muromachi* Era in the late sixteenth century, these secret groups were employed by a succession of Rulers and Warlords, but were unknown to the common people. It wasn't until the beginning of the *Sengoku* Era that the name of *Ninja* and the exploits of these Men of the Shadows came to the forefront and the Golden Age of the *Ninja* began.

After the fall of the *Muromachi* government, Japan became a nation of rebellion and wars. The country was broken up into small countries with Lords each trying to expand their boundaries. This brought about the total collapse of any kind of law and order. Robbery, murder, rape and the absence of morals and loyalties created a situation where only the strongest survived. In the midst of this chaos the *Ninja* came into his own.

For hundreds of years he had been available for hire as a necessity but now he was vital to the various Warlords, who needed to know the enemy's strength, and if and when he would attack, all this information had to be accurate and be available quickly.

In a land of chaos, the *Ninja* was a disciplined creature. In a country without morals, he was bound by a moral code that was almost saintly; where robbery, rape and killing were a daily occurence, he was devoid of greed and the passions of the flesh. He did kill, but only to order and without any personal feelings. He was a killing machine, that was available for hire, and, unthinkably, he was the only answer to the chaos that filled the *Sengoku* Era.

## Iga Ninja

For many hundreds of years the *Iga* Group of *Ninjas* had been the major force in *Ninjutsu*, though smaller groups had existed in other parts of Japan, but now *Ninja* Groups sprang up all over Japan. Within these special groups of spies, saboteurs and killers, there developed two Super Groups. The *Iga* Group of *Mie* prefecture and the deadly *Koga* Group of *Shiga* Prefecture, who specialised in poisons, fire sand (a kind of Gunpowder) and weapons.

Interestingly, *Shiga* Prefecture is next to *Mie* Prefecture in Southern Japan. The *Koga* and *Iga* Groups lived in the same mountain range, in two valleys divided by a mountain. Completely isolated from the outside world, they lived as farmers and were consulted by the locals on medicine, herbs, weather forcasting and agriculture.

From among the Warlords, great Generals came forth and gradually the unification of Japan came about. Great leaders such as *Takeda Shingen*, *Oda Nobunaga* and perhaps the greatest general in Japanese History, *Tokugawa Ieyasu* all employed the *Ninjas* to help control the country through a complex spy network manned by the *Ninjas*.

At one time *Nobunaga* developed a burning hatred against the *Iga* Group and sent an army in 1578 to teach them a lesson. When the army reached the *Iga* valley, the *Ninjas*, had disappeared. The soldiers destroyed the crops, burned the houses and set fire to the mountain. The following year, *Nobunaga* sent another army of eight thousand men into the valley of the *Iga*. The *Ninjas*, who had been hiding in the mountains, attacked the soldiers and drove them from the valley. In 1581, *Nobunaga* decided to kill every man, woman and child of the *Iga* Group and wipe them off the face of the earth. This time he sent fifty thousand soldiers, including other *Ninja* groups. With under four thousand *Ninjas*, the *Iga* Group fought a losing battle for a month and realising that they could not win, disbanded and

disappeared all over Japan. Several years passed and once more the *Iga* Group regrouped and smaller groups were formed in many areas of Japan.

After *Nobunaga* died (he was killed by unknown assassins?) *Tokugawa Ieyasu* became the Shogun and ruled over a united Japan.

The *Koga* Group had over the years developed strong ties with the Lords of Japan, having once rescued *Tokugawa Ieyasu* from an assassination attempt by rival *Ninjas*, were recruited by him when he became Shogun.

From 1600, the *Sengoku* Era ended and three hundred years of peace and prosperity followed, to be known as the *Tokugawa* Era in Japanese History. Up to this time the capital of Japan had been in *Kyoto*, but *Tokugawa Ieyasu* moved the capital to *Edo* or *Tokyo* as we now know it, and took with him three hundred *Ninjas* from the *Koga* and *Iga* Groups as personal bodyguards and later these *Ninjas* were used to guard the Castle of *Tokyo*.

Interestingly the *Koga Ninja* Group guarded the front gates of the Castle and the *Iga* guarded the back gates. However, in the living quarters of the Shogun, which housed the hundreds of women that made up the Shogun's court, the *Iga* guarded inside, while the *Koga Ninja* Group had to guard from the outside.

Now that peace had come at last to a united Japan, the *Ninja*, whose work and usefulness had been invaluable in times of war, found themselves made to act as glorified servants around the castle of *Tokyo*. They became known as *Oniwaban* (Gardeners) by the people and ridiculed by the *Samurai* and by the ladies-in-waiting who attended the court of the Shogun.

They were still sometimes used to gather information on any signs of rebellion and carried messages for the Lords, but mainly they acted as bodyguards to *Tokugawa Ieyasu*, vetting visitors who came to the castle.

As the years passed the *Ninjas* grew old and there were few young men willing to undergo the severe training needed to become a *Ninja*, so the Art of *Ninjutsu* died out in the middle of the seventeenth century. However, all the methods and techniques were written down and passed on in *Tora No Maki (Tiger Scrolls)* which have survived to this day.

*Just before the Second World War, a special group of men called the Tokubetsu Koto Keisatsu were formed and were said to have been trained in the Art of Ninjutsu.*

## IGA GROUP had 49 SUB-GROUPS
## KOGA GROUP had 53 FAMILY GROUPS
## IN ALL THERE WERE OVER 200 NINJA GROUPS

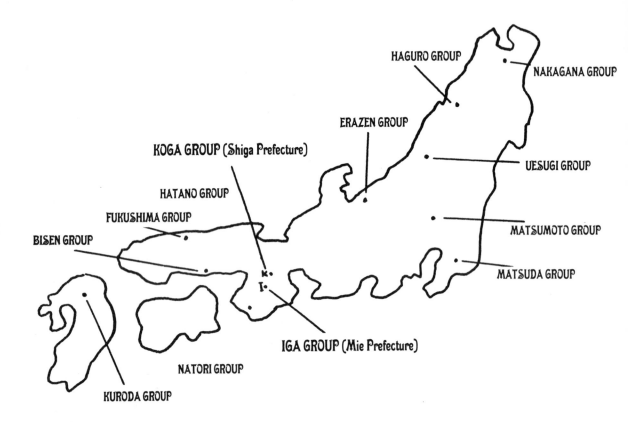

# 甲
# KO
## (KOGA NINJA)

## Koga Ryu Ninja

The *Koga* Group of *Ninja* lived in a valley among the mountains of *Shiga* Prefecture in Southern Japan. They consisted of fifty-three families and specialized in medicines, explosives and developed many of the tools and weapons used by the *Ninja*. Though small in number, they were an elite force and became the second most famous group in the annals of *Ninjitsu*. Based very near *Kyoto*, which was the capital of Japan at that time, they were recruited by the great rulers of Japan as councillors and military strategists.

In 1600 they made a dummy of the Lord *Tokugawa Ieyasu*, filled it with explosives and placed it in *Tokugawa's* carriage. They then acted as personal escort and made it known that *Ieyasu* was on the move through enemy territory. This diversionary tactic worked when the false carriage was attacked by the enemy and all the *Koga Ninja* were killed, giving the real carriage containing *Ieyasu* precious time to escape.

In 1614, after *Tokugawa Ieyasu* had become *Shogun* of a united Japan, a rebellion broke out led by *Toyotomi Hideyoshi*, who wanted to become the next Shogun after the death of *Ieyasu*. *Toyotomi* and his followers held *Osaka* Castle, which was impregnable and the siege by *Ieyasu's* army went on for over a month without any success. Then *Ieyasu* sent in a small group of *Koga Ninjas* and they began their *work* inside the Castle. First learning the enemy's strengths and weaknesses, which they sent to *Tokugawa Ieyasu*, they then began to cause discontent among the followers of *Toyotomi*. Dissention broke out in the army, strange sicknesses befell the inhabitants of the Castle and the people began to mysteriously die. After a few weeks, a message was sent to *Tokugawa Ieyasu* telling him to attack the Castle once again, which he did and *Toyotomi* was defeated.

The *Koga Ninja* Group was made up of three Ranks. The *Jonin* (High Rank), the *Chunin* (Middle Rank) and the *Genin* (Lower Rank).

## Jonin

These were the masters of the Groups, sometimes high officials in the government and personal friends of the great leaders. They were the men that accepted the commissions and worked out the plans and strategies to be employed in the various activities performed by the *Ninjas*. These they passed on to the *Chunin*.

## Chunin

These were the men responsible for the training and the discipline in the *Ninja* Groups. Each had his own sub-group and would decide who did what. If the orders were for attacks by large groups of men the *Chunin* would lead the attack. All the most famous *Ninjas* in History, men such as *Taroo, Kotaro* and *Kizaru* were all *Chunin*.

## Genin

The men that carried out the missions were the *Genin* or the Dark Spirits of the Night. These men in black, creeping over roof-tops, climbing up walls and appearing out of the darkness to cause mayhem and death were the faceless ones, without identity and willing to die rather than fail in a mission.

The qualifications needed to become a *Ninja* were needless to say impossible to be met by mere mortals, so usually a *Ninja* was born one, that is to say his family were *Ninjas* or, as a baby, his parents would give him to a *Ninja* group. Often, babies that had been abandoned were adopted by the groups and brought up to be a *Ninja*.

Here is a list of some of the qualifications needed to become a *Ninja*.
1) *Total Loyalty to your master, faithful and devoted to duty.*
2) *Brave, good at strategy and cunning, daring and trustworthy.*
3) *Intelligent, fullfil your obligations and never forget favours.*
4) *Able to think deeply and not easily deceived.*
5) *Total believer in Confucianism and Buddhism.*
6) *No personal desires of any kind, intuitive and even tempered.*
7) *Able to understand quickly and correctly any information given to you.*
8) *Obey and understand the code of Bushido (The Way of the Warrior)*
9) *The Morals of a Hero.*
10) *Love and Honour your family (Group) above all else.*

11) Never to betray your Group and always finish anything that you start.
12) Be well travelled and have knowledge of customs and people of all areas.
13) Believe that the Art Of *Ninjutsu* is superior to all others.
14) Be able to read, write, sing, dance and expert in mimicry.
15) Strong in body, good health and brilliant fighter.
16) Endure pain even unto death.

Once a man or woman became a *Ninja* there were *Five Rules* that had to be followed. Should any one of these rules be broken at any time, the *Ninja* would be killed by his Group.
1) At no time must you ever tell anyone that you are a *Ninja*.
2) All the methods you have learnt must never be taught to anyone.
3) When given an order, whatever it may be, it must be completed, even if that order was to kill a friend, a member of your own family or yourself, it must be carried out without question.
4) Never to divulge information regarding your mission or who hired you.
5) If you are captured and all means of escape have been tried and failed, you are to disfigure your own face to be totally unrecognisable or kill yourself.

## Tora No Maki (Tiger Scroll)

These contained the various exercises, techniques, tools, weapons, fighting strategies that were the Handbook of the *Ninja* and his Deadly Art of *Ninjutsu*. They were passed down by hand from Master to disciple, Teacher to student, Father to Son and were written in a complicated language of characters and symbols that only the *Ninja* could read or understand. Each Group had their own system of characters and symbols, so should these Scrolls be discovered or read by anyone who was not a *Ninja*, they would not be able to understand them.

Some of these Scrolls have survived to this day, handed down from one generation to another and now for the first time available in English.

# 忍
# NIN
# (NINJA, THE MAN)

## The Ninja

The *Ninja* was hired to perform *five* major functions: Spying; Reconnoitring; Carrying Secret Messages; Sabotage and Creating Confusion; Killing and Assassination.

### Spying

The most important work undertaken by the *Ninja* was spying. Secretly entering the enemy's Castle, he would gather information concerning the condition and morale of the soldiers, the weaknesses and strengths of the defences, the number of soldiers, their weapons and to learn of future plans and the possibility of forthcoming attacks or battles. Sometimes they would enter the Castle disguised as merchants, beggars, priests or entertainers and made friends with the enemy to gather the necessary information. The Female *Ninja* was especially effective in this area, gaining employment in the Castle and by listening to kitchen gossip, going to bed with the enemy soldiers and even sometimes marrying them to get the information.

### Reconniotring

The most dangerous work undertaken by the *Ninja* was reconnoitring. Before any major battle, they would infiltrate the enemy camps by joining up in the enemy's army. This would enable him to pass on vital information and the *Ninja* would continue this guise even into the actual fighting where they would sometimes be killed by the soldiers of the men who had employed them.

### Carrying Secret Messages

From an early age, the *Ninja* practiced running fast and over great distances and this ability made it possible for them to carry secret messages from one place to another in the shortest possible time. He sometimes carried false messages, which were intended to be captured by the enemy, giving their lives so that the message would be believed.

### Sabotage and Creating Confusion

During battles, small groups of *Ninjas* would attack the enemy, setting fire to the camps, coming from many directions at once to confuse the enemy regarding the strength and position of the opposing forces. Being recruited into the enemy's army they would lead the soldiers into traps, undermine the morale of the men by destroying weapons, killing them from the back and spreading rumours about traitors and encouraging soldiers to defect or desert.

## Killing and Assassination

With the *Ninja's* rigorous training, his vast knowledge of weapons, poisons and his ability to enter dwellings undetected and especially the cold efficiency with which he killed made him the perfect assassin.

# SHU
## (TRAINING)

# Training
# 'Preparation is All'

The training of a *Ninja* began from the age of eight years old. Before this, what the young child would receive would be instruction in reading, writing, mimicry of birds and animals and skills in throwing stones and climbing trees. when the child reached the age of eight his training would take on a new and more demanding form of practice. This new training was divided into three forms. *Shinren*, *Tairen* and *Chiren*.

## Shinren (Heart Training)

This form of practice involved the training of the senses and of instinct. The ability to see openings, to take chances when they appeared, to relax themselves in dangerous situations and to endure unbearable conditions such as heat, the cold, the wind, rain, hunger and thirst and finally pain. To read people's characters, to be able to instinctively understand every situation faced and deal with it immediately.

## Tairen (Body Training)

Building up and strengthening every part of the body, not to perform one function, but several, thereby multiplying the natural weapons possessed by man. To prepare the body so that it could fulfil the work that the *Ninja* would be called upon to perform and to take the punishment that would come and yet remain unbroken.

## Chiren (Knowledge Training)

In this form of training the *Ninja* would learn about strategy, medicines and poisons, explosives, weather forecasting, signalling, dialects, religion, farming, playing musical instruments, dancing, singing and psychology. In his disguises, he not only had to look like the person he was playing but also had to perform their work convincingly enough not to be found out.

## Ashi (Legs)

As the major part of a *Ninja's* work involved the

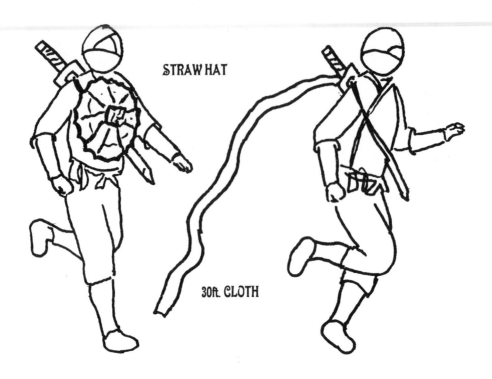

STRAW HAT

30ft. CLOTH

RUNNING ON PAPER

# FUTARIJINBA (Two Man Horse)

# SANNINJINBA (Three Man Horse)

carrying of messages over long distances and in the shortest possible time, entering castles and dwellings, climbing walls and over roof-tops, his legs had to have the strength to carry out these functions. As most of his life was living in forests, climbing over mountains, hiding in trees and moving over difficult terrain, the *Ninja* developed exercises to build up the speed and strength of his legs.

One method used to build up his speed was to tie a piece of cloth about thirty feet in length around his neck. The cloth hung down behind him and he would run as fast as he could without letting the end of the cloth touch the surface of the ground.

Another method used to build up his speed was to place a straw hat on his chest between his arms. He would run as fast as he could so that only the wind against the straw hat kept it firmly to his chest and stopped it falling to the ground.

All the running the *Ninja* had to do not only had to be fast or over great distances, but it all had to be done as quietly as possible. They placed pieces of paper on the ground and practiced running over the paper without tearing it. This was only possible by running on the toes.

Stamina training for the *Ninja* involved carrying heavy stones and rocks put inside sacks and these sacks were placed over the *Ninja's* shoulders and in bags around his waist. He would run over hills and rocky ground till he collapsed. The weights he had to carry were very heavy to begin with, but would gradually get lighter, which gave him the feeling that he was almost floating.

He could run between one hundred and one hundred and twenty kilometers in one day and at a speed of just under twenty kilometers per hour. A modern marathon runner, wearing just running shorts and vest, runs about fifty kilometres at twenty kilometres per hour whereas the *Ninja*, carrying all hs weapons and climbing equipment could run twice the distance.

They also practiced many different kinds of running such as running on tiptoes, on one leg in case he was wounded, running over wet surfaces, through water and a method that was often used, that of running sideways. The body was placed sideways with the leading shoulder slightly lowered for balance and direction. The feet crossed in front of each other. This method was used to run along beside a wall, along narrow passages by flattening the body against the wall, making it more difficult to be seen by the enemy.

## Tobu (Jumps)

Training included many kinds of jumps, as the *Ninja* had to be capable of jumping from roof to roof, jumping out of trees, over walls and down from high places. Jumps included forward jumping, high jumping, jumping with both feet together, diagonally and sideways.

## Futarijijba (Two Man Horse)

The *Ninja* had to sometimes jump over walls and on to roofs and to do this they had a special technique called a *Jinba*. The two-man *Jinba* consisted of one *Ninja* standing on the shoulders of a second *Ninja*. The *Ninja* underneath would run towards the wall and the other *Ninja* would crouch down ready to jump. As they reached the wall, the *Ninja* underneath would suddenly straighten up and at the same moment the *Ninja* on top would jump upwards. A very difficult manoeuvre involving timing and coordination between the two men, only made possible by hours of practice.

## Sanninjinba (Three Man Horse)

The three-man *Jinba* consisted of one *Ninja* standing with his back to the wall. A second *Ninja* would crouch down in front of the standing *Ninja*. A third *Ninja* would run towards the two *Ninjas* and with a motion similar to running upstairs, place his feet on the hands of the crouching *Ninja*. At the same time the standing *Ninja* would put his hands under the armpits of the third *Ninja* and with one continuous action, *Ninja* one and two would push up with all their strength and send the third *Ninja* up and on to the wall. From up on the wall the third *Ninja* would then pull up the other two *Ninjas*. This also required lots of practice to be successful.

## Heiko (Equilibrium)

As the places that the *Ninja* usually found himself were difficult to manoeuver in, balance was a very important part of their training. Working their way across high castle walls and over roof-tops in the darkness required a sure foot and safe balance. To develop this they used three methods.

They placed a long piece of bamboo from one tree to another. They would then, similar to a tightrope walker, cross the bamboo on their toes.

By wearing *Geta* (Japanese sandals with two slats of wood underneath to raise the wearer a few inches above the ground) with very high slats of wood and sometimes with one slat of wood they would walk over rocks and climb boulders.

SUNAMOCHI (Holding Sand)

TAKE IPPON (One Bamboo)

SACKS FILLED
WITH ROCKS

KAKEJIN
(Hanging Man)

Two bamboo poles would be placed across their shoulders. From the four ends of the bamboo poles, earthenware pots filled with water would be hung. The *Ninja* would then have to practice walking, running and turning with these heavy pots weighing him down. He wasn't allowed to spill a drop of water while executing these difficult manoeuvers.

## Te (Hand) Ude (Arm) Kata (Shoulder)

Entering dwellings, climbing up castle walls, hiding in trees not only required strength in the legs but also in the hands, arms and shoulders. Individual joints had to be developed into iron hooks, claws and the skin also had to be toughened.

The *Ninja* killed with his hands. He dug holes in the ground with his fingers. He scaled castle walls with his claws. To build up his hands to take this kind of punishment was an essential part of the *Ninja's* training. Should he find himself without his climbing equipment or his weapons, usually after he had successfully entered a dwelling and completed his mission, the *Ninja* would have the problem of escaping so he could not allow the loss of such equipment to hamper his flight. It could mean the difference between life and death.

The method used to toughen up the skin on his hands and to develop the strength in his wrists and fingers, the *Ninja* would stab with his outstretched fingers into a hole in the ground, first filled with sand, then rocks or stones would be added and finally pieces of metal were placed in these holes.

This changed his fingers into steel rods capable of penetrating a man's chest or smashing his skull.

Also by hitting trees with his fists and other parts of his hands he would develop the power of his strikes and punches. These techniques are used in modern day *Karate* but remember these secret hand toughening practices were used by the *Ninja* over a thousand years ago.

## Akuryoku (Gripping Power)

Not only was it necessary for the *Ninja* to build up the power in his strikes and punches but it was also vital that the *Ninja* had an iron grip needed for climbing and killing. The following three methods were used by the *Ninja* to create a grip that could break bones, crush wooden doors and even snap metal.

The *Ninja* would place his hands under water, then by repeatedly opening and closing the fingers he would develop his grip. This same exercise would be repeated using sand instead of water.

## Sunamochi (Holding Sand)

Clay pots filled with sand were gripped with the finger tips along the rims of the pots. These heavy pots would then be carried around for hours to develop an iron grip.

## Takeippon (One Bamboo)

Cut pieces of bamboo about three feet in length would be bound around a pole or the trunk of a tree. The *Ninja* would then have to pull out each bamboo with his fingers. This is a very painful form of training becsause the finger nails would usually be torn from the fingers as the individual bamboo was prised apart from the others.

## Kakejin (Hanging Man)

To build up the strength needed in his arms and shoulders, the *Ninja* would practise *Kakejin*. Sacks were filled with rocks or stones and were then placed over the *Ninja's* shoulders. Sacks were also tied around his waist and he would hang by the arms from the branch of a tree. He would remain in this position for as long as he could, building up to a point where he could endure this painful position for six to eight hours at a time. By totally relaxing and repeating a meditation chant, he was able to place his weight in his head and lighten himself.

## Musubi (Tying Up)

If a *Ninja* was caught and tied up, it was imperative that he escape as soon as possible and to be able to do this the *Ninja* learned to manipulate his joints. From an early age, as their bodies were growing, the *Ninja* would dislocate the joints in their fingers, wrists, shoulders, hips, knees and ankles. This would make him double-jointed and he therefore could hide in small or narrow places. When being pursued by the enemy, the *Ninja* would dig a hole in the earth and hide in it. To enter a castle, they would also hide in boxes and trunks and were carried into the castle with the luggage. When engaged in un-armed combat with the enemy, which at that time was *Jujutsu*, which used locks and joint holds, the *Ninja* could easily defeat the enemy and escape.

This training of dislocating the joints and setting them himself was an extremely painful form of practice that the *Ninja* underwent as often the joints would develop arthritis and the *Ninja* would live the rest of his life in terrible pain.

Because this form of training was used by all the *Ninja* Groups, they developed a secret method of tying up a rival *Ninja* so that he could not escape.

The first knot was always made around both thumbs placed in a criss-cross position. It was then pulled very tightly and the arms were tied around the back of the person and ended either around the neck or tied around the two big toes. Tied up in this way it is impossible to escape as the bone between the first and second joint of the thumb is very narrow in the middle compared to the ends of the joint.

## Mudo (Stillness)

The most severe of all the different methods of training practiced by the *Ninja*, was the method of doing nothing. Once a *Ninja* had entered a castle or dwelling, he would find a place to hide and then have to remain there until the information that he had been sent to get had been gathered or the person he had been sent to kill was dead. This could be hours, days and sometimes even longer and therefore it was imperative that the *Ninja* remain as still as possible as any sound might give away his presence and result in his death.

To be as quiet as possible meant that he would have to control his breathing. To overcome the sound of his breath, the *Ninja* learnt not to breathe so often. He regulated his breathing to the extent that he took one breath every two minutes and by placing a small piece of cotton in each nostril, the actual volume of breath intake and exhalation was greatly reduced. This also helped to muffle the sound of the breath.

The *Ninja* could not carry too much food or water with him, so he would have to go without nourishment for days. This was accomplished by the *Ninja* learning to sit or stand still for hours, even days and food and water was placed in front of him. He would also practice this denial of basic nourishments next to a river or members of his group would sit in front of him eating and drinking.

## HEIKO PRACTICE

GETA

EARTHENWARE POTS

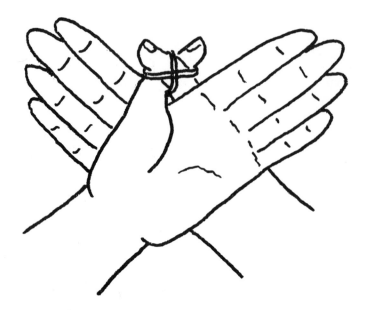

CROSS-THUMB TIE

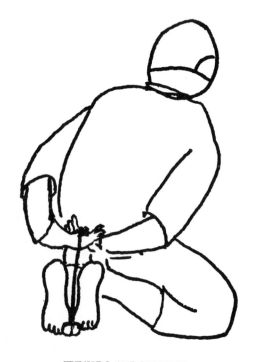

THUMBS AND BIG TOES

MUDO (Stillness)

ZAZEN (Sitting Meditation)

武

# BU

## (WEAPONS)

# Weapons

The *Ninja* was a soldier and like all soldiers, he carried a weapon for attack and defence. However, unlike an ordinary soldier, who specialises in a single weapon that fulfills a single function, the *Ninja's* weapons had to have three requirements to suit his kind of warfare.

As a secret soldier, who had to travel fast and silently, the weapons that he carried had to be concealable, portable and most importantly had to be flexible. Each weapon was designed to have a myriad of uses and the *Ninja* had to be able to use them with skill, as his way of life depended on him never being vulnerable in any situation.

Usually working alone, they only had themselves to rely on and the responsibility they carried, gathering information, delivering secret messages and assassinations did not allow for failure of any kind.

In the age that the *Ninja* existed, most soldiers carried a sword or *Katana* at all times as a basic weapon, to defend themselves or to administer justice. To the *Samurai*, his sword was his right hand, his family heirloom, his soul and as a very expensive piece of hardware was not available to the general public. At certain times they were forbidden to carry a sword, so most people carried a wooden weapon, usually a staff and sometimes a small knife in the belt.

## Shinobigatana (Secret Sword)

The *Samurai* Sword or *Katana* had but one function, that was to cut, and in their training most techniques centred around cutting movements. Blocks or parries were not encouraged as this might damage or mark these precious blades.

The Sword carried by the *Ninja* was the *Shinobigatana* and unlike the *Samurai* Sword had a multi-

# SHINOBIGATANA
## (Secret Sword)

TSUBA (Guard)

SAGEO (Cord)

SAYA (Scabbard)

SAND, PEPPER
METAL SHAVINGS

DETACHABLE TIP

tude of uses plus the obvious one of cutting. The *Ninja's* Sword was shorter, about fifty centimetres and was carried across the back with the hilt sticking out above the right shoulder. This was so that it was easier for the *Ninja* to scale walls or climb trees without it getting in his way. It was drawn with the right hand over the right shoulder.

Attached to the *Saya* (Scabbard) was a *Sageo* (cord or rope) which was about twelve foot long and had a large, square-shaped *Tsuba* (guard), unlike the *Samurai* Sword, which has a small, oval-shaped guard.

The *Shinobigatana* was used in *Five* different Ways.

1) When the *Ninja* wanted to climb over a wall to enter a dwelling, he would lean the sword against the wall and holding the *Sageo* (Cord) between his teeth; he would stand on the large, square-shaped *Tsuba* (guard) and climb on to the wall. He would then pull the sword after him by the cord.

2) When confronted by the enemy with a spear or surrounded by several men, he would hold the *Sageo* (Cord) and swing the *Saya* (Scabbard) around his head, as a way of driving off the enemy.

3) When moving silently through a dwelling or room in the darkness, it would be impossible to see or hear if there were anyone else in the room. The *Ninja* would hold the *Sageo* (cord) between his teeth, the blade of the sword would be about three-quarters of its length out of the *Saya* (Scabbard) and held in the right hand. The scabbard would be held out in front of the *Ninja* as he moved forward, probing the darkness. When the end of the scabbard came into contact with the enemy, the *Ninja* would let the scabbard fall to the ground and with his now exposed blade, stab or cut into the darkness.

4) The *Ninja* always carried sand, peppers and metal shavings at the bottom of his *Saya* (Scabbard). After he had drawn his sword, he would swing the scabbard and the contents would fly out into the faces of the enemy.

5) The tip of the *Saya* (Scabbard) could also be detached and the scabbard used as a blowpipe or as a snorkle for breathing under water.

## Sageo (Cord or Rope)

The *Sageo* of a *Samurai* Sword was used to secure the scabbard to the side of the *Samurai's Obi* (Belt), but the *Ninja's Sageo*, being much longer was used in many different ways.

1) When a *Ninja* was being pursued, either through a house or in the forest, he would tie the cord across a doorway or between two trees, to trip up his pursuers.

2) Often the *Ninja* would have to live out in the open, under all kinds of conditions, so by tying the *Sageo* over a bush in a spiders web shape and placing leaves over it, it acted as a tent or shelter against the elements.

3) High up in the top branches of a tree, where the *Ninja* might be hiding, he would erect a kind of hammock with the cord so he could rest or sleep.

4) If he was wounded, he could use the cord as a tourniquet to stop the bleeding.

5) The cord could also be used to tie up people, if it were not necessary to kill them.

## Tabiumi (Travel Bow)

When a *Ninja* was in disguise, as a priest or traveller, he could not carry his usual deadly array of weapons in case he was stopped by the *Samurai* or was searched. As he made his way along the roads or passed through villages and towns, he always had with him a concealed weapon known as a *Tabiumi*. It was about half the size of a normal bow and by means of a metal joint in the middle of the bamboo, could be folded in half and carried in a sack or hidden in the clothing the *Ninja* was wearing.

If this was too dangerous, he would only carry the string and out of a piece of bamboo quickly make up a bow. However the arrows, tipped with poison, were vital and had to be always readily available. The arrows were concealed under his straw hat. They sometimes were used to make up the straw hat by acting as ribs to support the straw covering.

The arrows were about twenty-five centimetres long and flighted with paper or bird feathers. Unlike the long bow, the *Tabiumi* had a short range and was usually effective up to twenty yards, but as the tips were poisoned, capable of killing a person.

## Shuriken (Behind Hand Knife)

The perfect weapon for an Assassin would have to be small, light, easy to conceal and deadly. The *Ninja* possessed such a weapon. The *Shuriken* filled these requirements perfectly, being very light and small. The *Ninja* carried about his person a variety of these deadly weapons in many shapes and sizes.

# SHINOBI GATANA (Secret Sword)

SWINGING
AROUND OVER HEAD

CLIMBING

PROBING THE DARKNESS

**KASA (Straw Hat)**

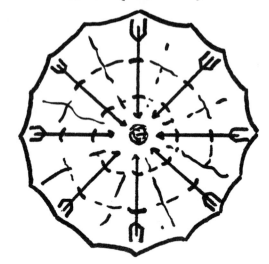

**TABIYA (Travel Arrows)**

**TABIUMI (Travel Bow)**

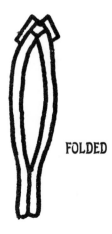

FOLDED

They were usually to be thrown at the enemy to distract his attention or make him flinch, and in that moment the *Ninja* would draw his sword and strike the enemy. It was also used to slow up the enemy while the *Ninja* made his escape.

Effective up to about fifteen feet as a wounding weapon, but when the tip was covered with poison, death could occur from infection. The *Shuriken* was also used as a knife and the needle-like blade buried deep into the neck or chest of the victim.

Originally a long needle-shaped missile from six to eight inches long, pointed at one end, it was instantly taken out and thrown at the enemy. It required a great deal of practice to make the *Shuriken* strike the enemy point first. Over the years, many shapes of *Shuriken* were invented and were easier to throw and hit the mark. These included the *Juji* (Cross), *Manji* (Swastika), *Happo* (Star), *Sampo* (Triangle), *Taira* (Flat) and the *Tatamijuji* (Folding Cross).

## Shuriken Mochikata (Holding the Shuriken)

Unlike the western dart, which is weighted at the pointed end and flighted to make it fly true, the *Shuriken* was evenly weighted and therefore required a secret method of holding to ensure that the point struck first and not hit the target at an angle, thereby reducing its power and effectiveness.

The *Shuriken* was held in the palm of the hand with the thumb holding it firmly in place. It would lie along the outstretched fingers between the first and middle fingers. If the distance to be thrown was to be a long one, the *Shuriken* would be held deeper into the palm of the hand.

## Shuriken Nagekata (Throwing the Shuriken)

The *Shuriken* was thrown with a cutting motion, starting from the shoulder, through the arm and ending at the finger tips.

## Masugu (Straight) Kaiten (Turn)

The *Shuriken* could be thrown so that the point always remained the leading edge or it could be turned in an 180 degree spin. To be thrown in *Masugu*, the point would be facing out, if the *Shuriken* was to be thrown in *Kaiten*, then the point would be facing back and held in place by the thumb.

## Omote (Front) Yoko (Side) Gyaku (Reverse)

The *Shuriken* was thrown from three directions; *Omote*, *Yoko* and *Gyaku*. The front throw was the easiest and had the most power behind it. The side and reverse throws were not so powerful but they were difficult to see and therefore had the added advantage of surprise. From these three directions the *Shuriken* could either be thrown straight or do a half turn.

## Ichi (Position)

The *Shuriken* was practiced so that it could be thrown from any position. Standing, running, kneeling, sitting, lying on the front, lying on the back and also being able to throw two *Shuriken* at once in different directions were practiced.

Many *Shuriken* had a small hole in the centre, which had nothing to do with aerodynamics, but were in fact used to carry the various *Shuriken* in large numbers. A piece of rope was passed through the holes and tied around the waist.

The *Shuriken* was also use to start a fire. The *Ninja* would rub two metal *Shuriken* together and make a spark to be used to set off his explosives.

## Arare (Hailstones)

A three-dimensional *Shuriken* called the *Arare* looked very much like a spiked ball and when thrown had a one hundred percent chance to strike the target and was therefore a terrifying weapon. It was made in three sizes to be used in three different ways. The *Joarare* (Large Hailstones) was used by the *Ninja* to throw at wooden doors or on to the roofs of houses. A piece of cloth was tied around the spiked ball and set on fire.

The *Chuarare* (Medium Hailstones) were used as a throwing weapon similar to the *Shuriken*. The *Kaoarare* (Small Hailstones) were left on the ground or thrown at the feet of pursuers to slow them down.

## Metsubushi (Eye Closer)

Another throwing weapon that the *Ninja* carried was a *Metsubushi*. They were paper bags filled with sand, pepper and metal shavings and were thrown at the face of the enemy. On impact the paper bags would burst and instantly cause the eyes of the enemy to water profusely or even blind them. The *Ninja* sometimes carried this deadly mixture in empty shells of a bird's eggs and threw them at the enemy.

# SHURIKEN (Behind Hand Knife)

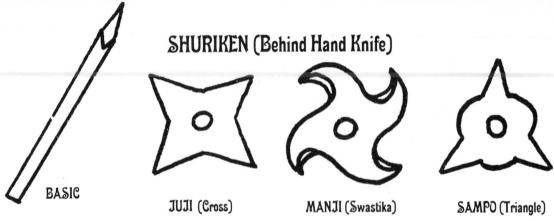

**BASIC**

**JUJI (Cross)**

**MANJI (Swastika)**

**SAMPO (Triangle)**

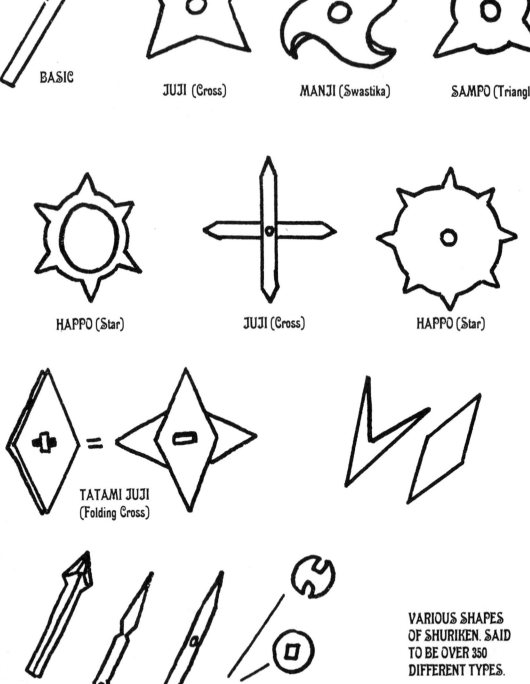

**HAPPO (Star)**

**JUJI (Cross)**

**HAPPO (Star)**

**TATAMI JUJI
(Folding Cross)**

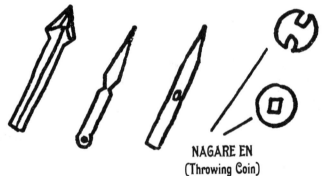

**NAGARE EN
(Throwing Coin)**

VARIOUS SHAPES
OF SHURIKEN. SAID
TO BE OVER 350
DIFFERENT TYPES.

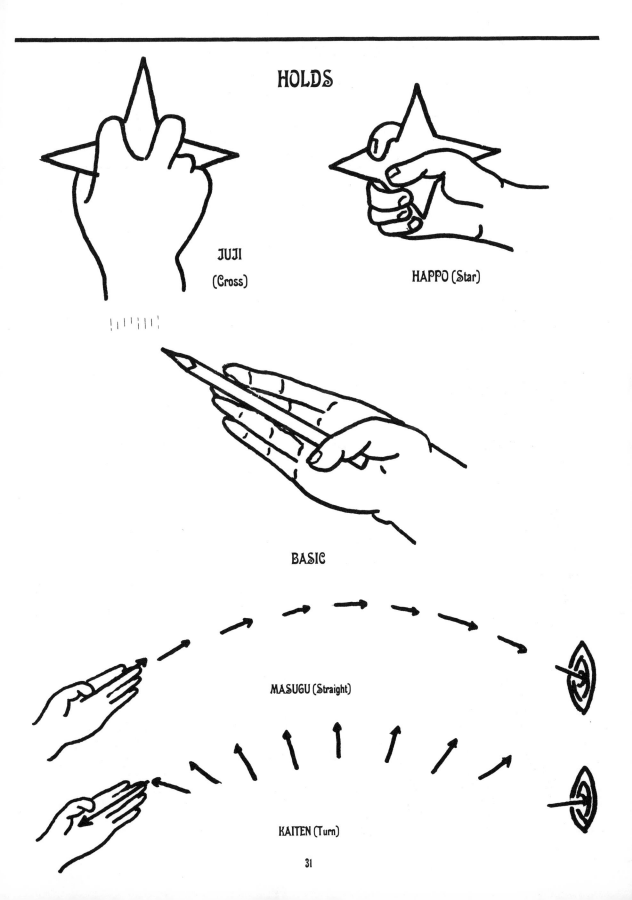

# HOLDS

JUJI
(Cross)

HAPPO (Star)

BASIC

MASUGU (Straight)

KAITEN (Turn)

## Fukibari (Spitting Needles)

Even smaller *Shuriken* or more correctly *Hari* (Needles) were carried by the *Ninja* in their mouths. They were about two inches long and were usually used for sewing and making *Tatami* mats.

Two methods of using the *Fukibari* were practiced. Both highly dangerous, not only to the enemy but also for the *Ninja* himself. Often the tips of the needles had been covered with poison and should the *Ninja* swallow them, he would certainly die a slow and agonising death.

1) The first method of using the *Fukibari* was to put a single needle in the mouth in the centre of the tongue. By curling the edges of the tongue inwards to make a tube shape and by blowing hard, the needle would shoot out into the face of the enemy.

2) The second method was to conceal a bamboo tube, with half a dozen needles inside it, in the mouth. When it was needed the *Ninja* would bring the bamboo tube to his lips and blow, like a blow-pipe, and the needles would spray out.

With practice it was possible to reach a distance of not more than twenty feet, but like the *Shuriken*, it was usually used as a diversionary tactic before a strike or when making an escape.

## Fukiya (Blow Darts)

Another blowing weapon that the *Ninja* used was the *Fukiya*. This was a blowpipe about thirty centimetres long and made of bamboo that was light and easy to carry. As the force of the blow was not very powerful, the *Ninja* aimed at vital parts, such as the eyes, throat, forehead and side of the neck. The tips of these darts were coated with poison, so even a small penetration would cause unconsciousness and death.

As it could be used from a hidden position and was silent, it was a favourite weapon of the *Ninja* to get past guards or for killing.

The blowpipe was usually a piece of bamboo but sometimes the *Ninja* used a rolled up piece of paper to form the tube or pipe.

The darts were made in the shape of cones and a kind of paper was the material used. At the pointed end of the cone dart, three needles coated with poison were tied. Another kind of cone dart had a piece of wire attached to the end of the cone and off from the wire, reverse spikes were used so that once the point had penetrated the skin, it was difficult to pull out.

The blowpipe was also used to pass messages. The information would be written on the paper cone and the dart shot high into the trees to be found later by fellow *Ninjas*.

Up to this point all the weapons used by the *Ninja* have been long distance mayhem, i.e. throwing, shooting and blowing. Perhaps the most difficult method of fighting or killing a man is close-combat, as the assailant gets to not only see the face of the opponent but also sees the effect of his attack.

The following weapons were more terrifying than the others, insomuch as they were fearsome in appearance and the damage they inflicted on their unsuspecting victims left wounds and scars that would be carried all their lives. These weapons were used by the *Ninja* for the psychological effect that they had on their enemies.

When a *Ninja* jumped out of the darkness or down from a tree, just the sight of these weapons was usually enough to make the enemy turn and run.

## Tekkokagi (Hand Claw)

They were made of metal and worn on the hand resembling the claws of a bear. There were two kinds, one worn on the back of the hand and one worn in the palm of the hand. The thickest piece of metal was shaped around the hand and attached to it were four long curved hooks. The *Tekkokagi* worn in the palm of the hand was used to deflect a sword cut or block, and the *Ninja* would slap at the enemy's face or head, where the long metal hooks would rip the flesh and crush the skull, causing death or more often than not, inflicting a terrible, unrepairable wound.

Like all weapons that the *Ninja* carried, it could also be used for climbing castle walls and trees.

## Nekkote (Cat's Paws)

The *Nekote* were five metal hooks, that were worn around the ends of the fingers and thumb. The tips of the hooks had poison smeared on them and they were used with a slashing movement. It did not have the same capabilities as the *Tekkokagi*, such as blocking swords and climbing, but its effect on the enemy was equally terrifying.

# THROWING METHODS

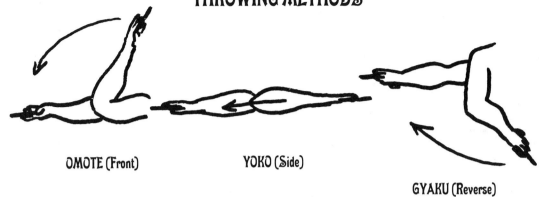

OMOTE (Front)    YOKO (Side)

GYAKU (Reverse)

# THROWING POSITIONS

STANDING    SITTING    LYING (Front)    LYING (Back)    TWO DIRECTION THROW

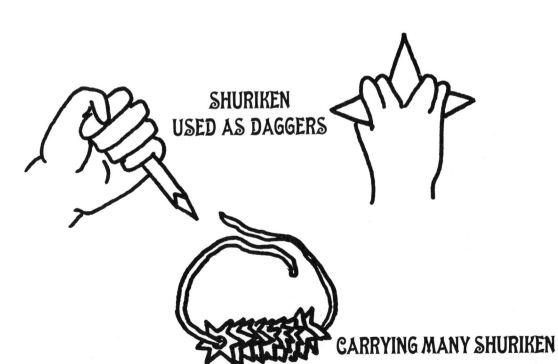

SHURIKEN
USED AS DAGGERS

CARRYING MANY SHURIKEN

# ARARE (Hailstones)

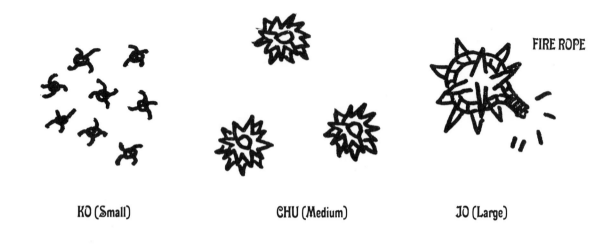

FIRE ROPE

KO (Small)　　　　CHU (Medium)　　　　JO (Large)

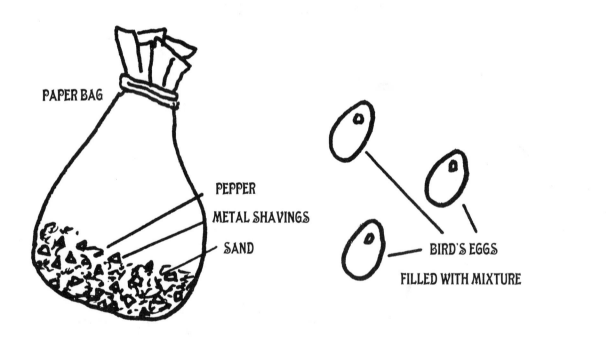

PAPER BAG

PEPPER

METAL SHAVINGS

SAND

BIRD'S EGGS

FILLED WITH MIXTURE

# METSUBUSHI (Eye Closer)

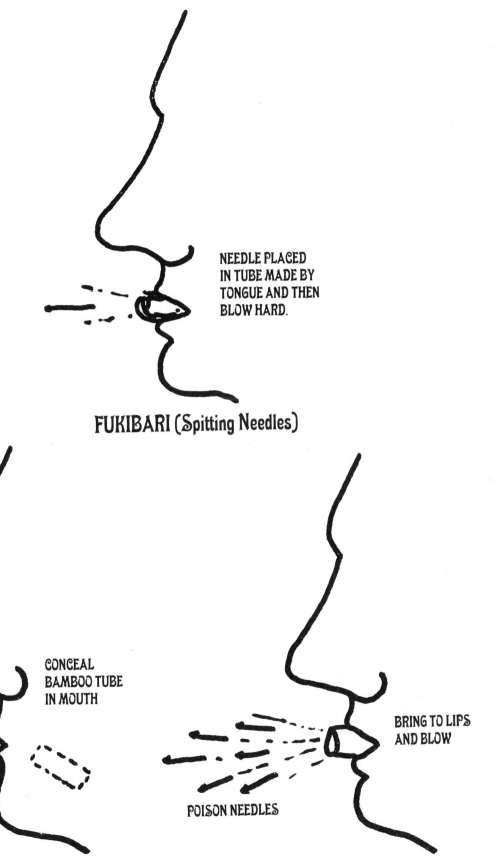

NEEDLE PLACED IN TUBE MADE BY TONGUE AND THEN BLOW HARD.

## FUKIBARI (Spitting Needles)

CONCEAL BAMBOO TUBE IN MOUTH

BRING TO LIPS AND BLOW

POISON NEEDLES

## Tekkon (Iron Hand)

This was a curved piece of metal worn around the hand, similar to a modern day knuckle-duster, and was used in the same way as the *Tekkokagi* to block swords, but as it was worn on the back of the hand could also add power to a bone crushing punch.

## Kakute (Horn Finger)

The *Kakute* was a ring of metal worn around the middle finger. It had two needle-like horns coated with poison attached to the ring and when worn facing outwards, made a punch a killing blow. Usually worn on the inside, that is to say, with the horns pointing out through the palm of the hand, it became an undetected weapon of death.

In a fight it only needed the *Ninja* to grab a wrist or ankle for the horns to penetrate the skin and the poison to do its work. This was a favourite weapon of the *Kunoichi*, the female *Ninja*, looking to all intents and purposes like an ordinary ring, she could carry it wherever she went and was particularly effective in bed.

In ancient Japan, women were always brought to the bed of a *Samurai* or an official completely naked, this was to make sure that she wasn't carrying any concealed weapons. The female *Ninja*, wearing nothing but her ring, would not appear to be a threat and during the lovemaking, she would put her hand behind the man's neck and the two poison coated needles would pierce the skin. She could grab any part of his body and the result would be the same, a slow agonizing death.

## Kusari (Chain) Kusarigama (Chain and Cutter)

The *Ninja* sometimes carried a *Kusari*, but this was not particular to the *Ninja*, as the *Samurai* and also peasants carried this weapon. It was a long piece of chain with two heavy pieces of metal at each end of the chain. It was swung around and used either to strike an enemy or to entangle his arms or legs. The rolled up piece of chain could also be held inside a closed hand and then suddenly flicked out into the face of the enemy.

A *Kama* (Grass cutter) was sometimes attached to the chain and was called a *Kusarigama*. Used in the same way as the piece of chain, but whereas the *Kusari* needed a sword or a knife to finish off the enemy, with the *Kama* attached, this was used to cut the enemy's throat. The *Kama* was also used to cut wood or dig holes when the necessity arose.

## Gyokagi (Fish Hook Cane) Shinobi-jo (Secret Cane)

When the *Ninja* was disguised as a traveller, he would have with him a walking stick. At that time most people who travelled carried a stick, but unlike the innocent walking stick of a real traveller, the *Ninja's* cane concealed various deadly attachments.

The *Gyokagi* concealed a long piece of string with a hook at the end. This was hidden in the bamboo cane and secured by a stopper. By flicking the cane, the hook would fly out and catch an unsuspecting victim and pull him down off a wall. Needles to say it was also used for fishing.

The *Shinobijo* was made from a piece of bamboo about three feet in length. At one end of the hollow cane, the *Ninja* would store his poison tipped needles and to keep them from falling out, a cap was placed on the end of the walking stick. At the other end of the cane a blade would be fitted into a narrow slit and could be exposed by a hard flick of the walking stick. This was used in a slashing motion or could be used to hook an arm, a foot or a neck.

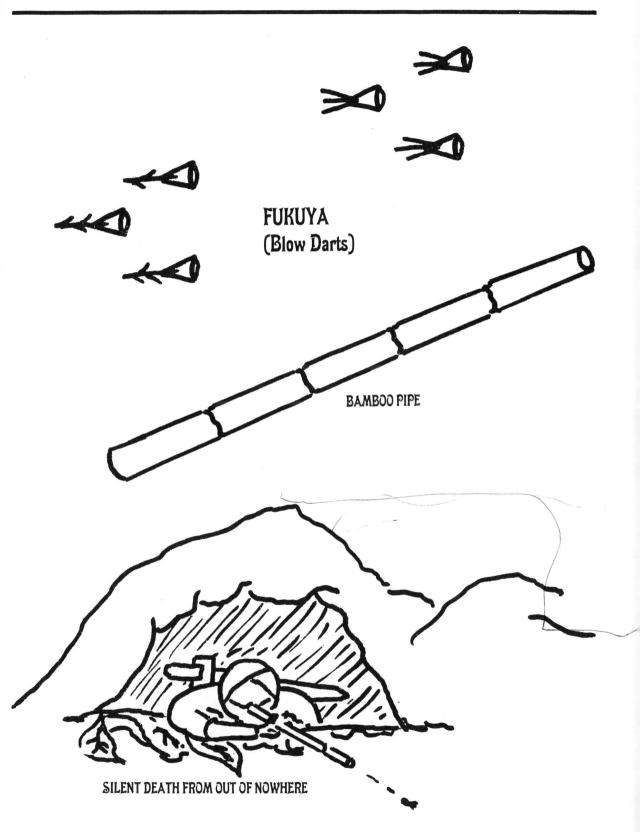

FUKUYA
(Blow Darts)

BAMBOO PIPE

SILENT DEATH FROM OUT OF NOWHERE

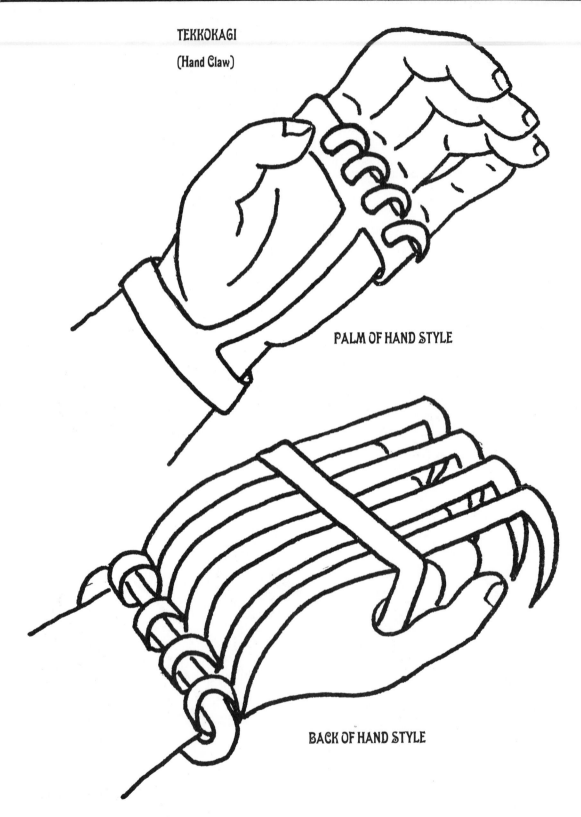

TEKKOKAGI

(Hand Claw)

PALM OF HAND STYLE

BACK OF HAND STYLE

NEKOTE (Cat's Paws)

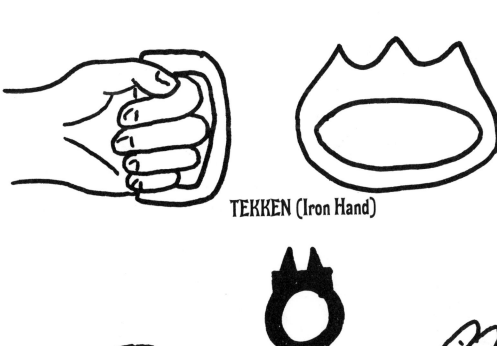

TEKKEN (Iron Hand)

KAKUTE
(Horn Finger)

WORN ON OUTSIDE

WORN ON INSIDE

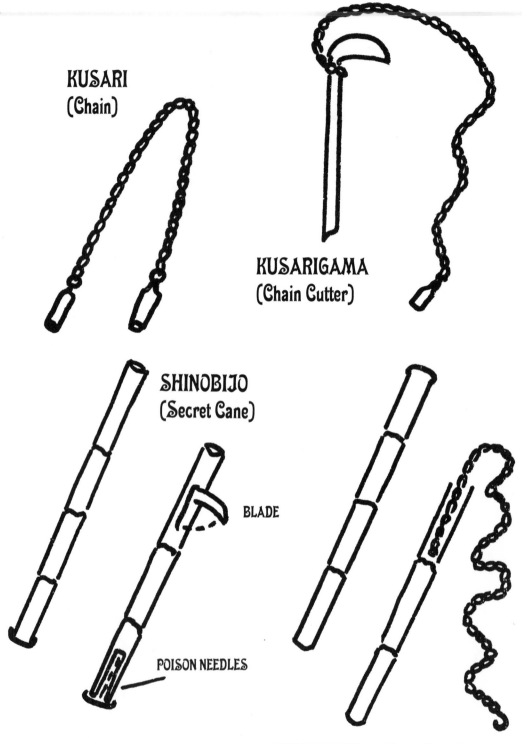

KUSARI
(Chain)

KUSARIGAMA
(Chain Cutter)

SHINOBIJO
(Secret Cane)

BLADE

POISON NEEDLES

GYOKAGI (Fish Hook Cane)

# 具

# GU

## (TOOLS)

# Equipment

## Shinobifuku (Secret Outfit)

During the day, as the *Ninja* travelled, he would be disguised as a priest, traveller or beggar but when he worked at night, under cover of darkness, he wore the *Shinobifuku*. The colour was a very dark brown, not black as popularly represented and was made up of three pieces of cloth. One piece was worn as a jacket that covered his chest, back and arms. The other two pieces were wound around each leg and tied at the waist making it easy to take off separately. These pieces of cloth were used as protection against the elements when he made camp and were used like a tent. The cloth could also be used to support him as he floated across a river on his back as he could tie one end around his neck and by scooping the air, fill it up like a life-jacket.

On the reverse side of this dark brown cloth would be a different colour, depending on the type of terrain he would have to cross and the weather conditions. The reverse colour could be white, if it were winter and he had to cross snow covered ground or the colour would be green if he were to travel through grasslands or hide in the forest.

## Zukin (Hood)

Wound around his head was a *Zukin*, which was a six foot long piece of cloth and it was wrapped around his head to that just the area around his eyes would remain uncovered. This cloth was soaked with sap from special plants and used to bind wounds and would stop infection developing while the *Ninja* was on a mission. It was also used to strain water from dirty rivers for drinking and when wet and heavy could be swung around the head and used as a weapon.

## Kusuribin (Medicine Can) Tsukedake (Bamboo Container)

In his *Obi* (Belt) he would carry a *Kusuribin* to carry his medicines and poisons. A *Tsukedake* was used to carry metal shavings, pepper and his Seed of Fire (Gunpowder). Gunpowder had come to Japan during the sixteenth century and was a favourite weapon of the *Ninja*. At that time a very unpredictable weapon, deadly to both user and enemy alike and therefore needed someone with nerves of steel to use it.

## Sekihitsu (Stone Pencil)

He also carried a *Sekihitsu*, which was a long piece of stone, used for writing messages on stones or trees to be discovered later by other members of his Group. It was also used like a *Shuriken* when thrown or held in the hand like a knife.

## Kaginawa (Rope Hook)

Attached to his belt was a *Kaginawa*, which was a basic climbing tool for climbing trees and scaling up walls.

Last but not least, he would have his *Shinobigatana* (Secret Sword), worn across the back with the hilt sticking up over the right shoulder. This was secured across the front of the chest by the *Sageo* (Cord).

## Waraji (Straw Sandal)

On his feet the *Ninja* wore *Waraji* with cords made of straw binding them around his feet, ankles and criss-crossed up his leg and tied off above the calves of his legs. These *Waraji* were worn by most people at that time when they travelled, but the *Ninja*, who had to travel fast over difficult terrain, tied pieces of metal with a spiked edge under the straw sandals, giving himself a better grip over uneven surfaces and also extra speed when he ran. This idea is the same used nowadays by athletes who wear spikes under their running shoes or sportsmen who have studs under their boots.

All footwear leave footprints on the ground and the *Ninja* could by counting the footprints know of large troop movements or well travelled roads to steer clear of but his footprints could also be read by the enemy so the *Ninja* would attach pieces of different shaped wood under the *Waraji* to confuse the enemy.

These shapes could be like animal footprints or the shape of sandals facing backwards or give the impression of a one-legged man, a cripple, fat, small or large people. Also shapes that had no recognisable shape, so that the enemy would think that nobody had crossed an area of ground or open grasslands.

The *Ninja* equipment or tools can be divided into five different areas: Weapons; Fire; Water; Climbing tools; Opening tools.

# SHINOBIFUKU (Secret Outfit)

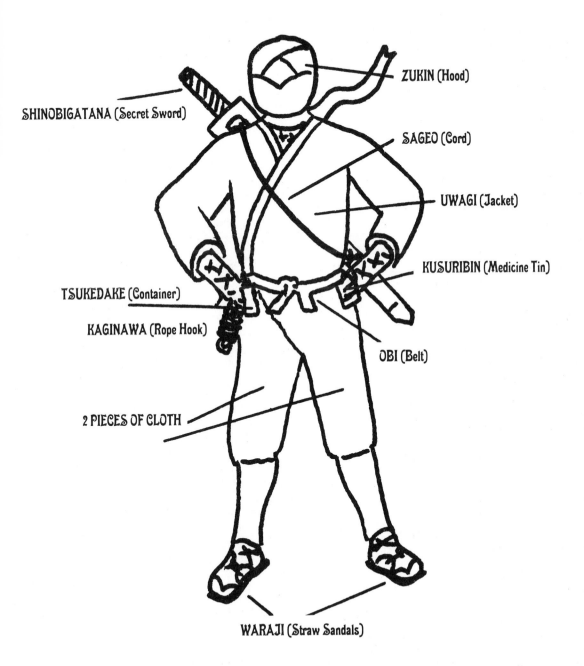

ZUKIN (Hood)

SHINOBIGATANA (Secret Sword)

SAGEO (Cord)

UWAGI (Jacket)

KUSURIBIN (Medicine Tin)

TSUKEDAKE (Container)

KAGINAWA (Rope Hook)

OBI (Belt)

2 PIECES OF CLOTH

WARAJI (Straw Sandals)

ZUKIN (Hood)

TSUKEDAKE (Bamboo Container)

KUSURIBIN (Medicine Tin)

SEKIHITSU (Stone Pen)

KAGINAWA (Rope Hook)

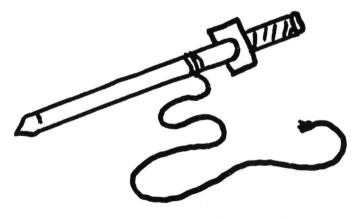

SHINOBIGATANA (Secret Sword)

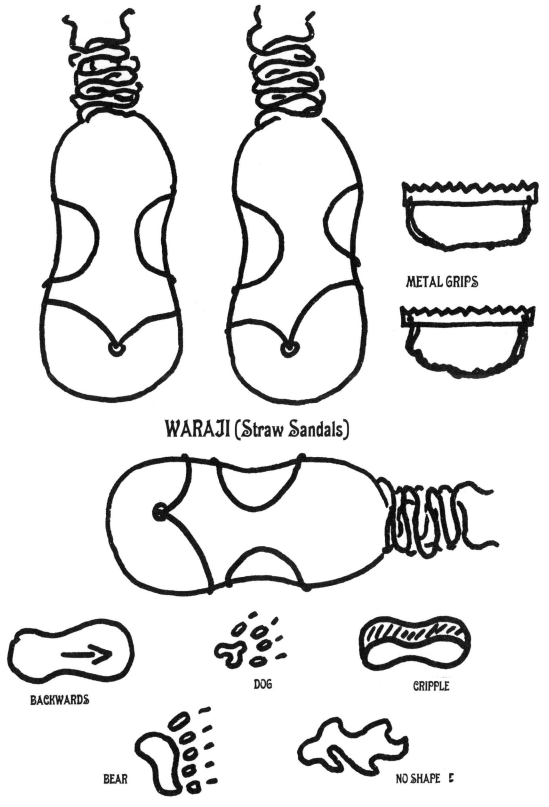

METAL GRIPS

WARAJI (Straw Sandals)

BACKWARDS

DOG

CRIPPLE

BEAR

NO SHAPE

ASHIATO (Footprints)

## Kaki (Fire tools)

As the weapons have already been dealt with earlier, let us look at the second area, that of Fire, which could also be under the same heading as weapons. At a time when all the houses were made of wood and paper and fire-fighting equipment had not been invented, the most terrifying hazard that the people of ancient Japan lived with was fire. The *Ninja* knew this and used their fire weapons to cause confusion, to set alight dwellings and for killing.

## HIYA (Fire Arrow) HIJO (Fire Sticks) HIDAKE (Fire Bamboo) HIKYU (Fire Ball) TORINOKO (Bird's Eggs)

The *Hiya* were tubes made of paper filled with gunpowder and were attached to the arrows. These were then fired into castles and on to roof tops. The *Hijo* was a piece of stick, pointed at both ends and a ball of paper wrapped around the middle. The paper was set alight and thrown like a *Shuriken* into houses. The *Hidake* was a bamboo, filled with gunpowder and once set alight, thrown into the enemy camps to frighten the horses, set the camp ablaze and cause chaos among the enemy soldiers before or during a battle. The *Hikyu* was made from two pieces of earth, baked into two halves of a ball. The hollow insides were filled with gunpowder and tied together into a ball with a rope. The *Torinoko* were the empty shells of bird's eggs filled with gunpowder and thrown in the same way as the *Hikyu* and *Hidake*.

## Suiki (Water Equipment)

The Castles in ancient Japan were similar to castles found in Europe, in so much as they were surrounded by water as an added defence against attacks, and as *Japan* is a land criss-crossed by thousands of rivers, the crossing of water was a major obstacle to be overcome by the *Ninja*. Rafts and boats for crossing over water, equipment for floating and carrying weapons across water and methods of travelling and hiding under water were researched and developed by the *Ninja*.

## Shinobibune (Secret Boat) Kameikada (Tortoise Raft) Kameikada (Jar Raft)

Various methods of crossing water included the Secret Boat. This was made from bamboo sticks and covered with bark from trees. The secret of this boat was the fact that it was made up of three different sections, which made it easy to carry or hide and could be quickly assembled when needed.

The *Kameikada* was made by tying pieces of bamboo in a criss-cross shape and between the spaces of the bamboo sticks, tortoise shells were tied with straw cords. Another raft was called a *Kameikada*. (In Japanese writing there are two different characters which, when spoken are pronounced, '*Kame*' but when written are a different set of lines. One means a Tortoise and the other means a jar or pot.) This was also made by tying pieces of bamboo in a criss-cross shape but instead of tortoise shells, half filled jars of water were secured between the sticks.

## Mizukakigeta (Web Sandal)

For swimming under water the *Ninja* used a *Mizukakigeta*, which was a piece of flat wood attached underneath their *Geta* sandals. This would give extra strength to the kicking of the feet as they swam. What we now know as flippers were being used in Japan over a thousand years ago.

## Mizugumo (Water Spider)

Perhaps the most famous piece of equipment used by the *Ninja* for crossing water was the *Mizugumo*. This was made from five pieces of wood. Four pieces were cut in an arc shape and tied together at the ends. The fifth piece of wood was cut in a flat rectangular shape and placed in the centre of the circle created by the other four pieces of wood. All the pieces were tied together in a spider web shape and the *Ninja* would stand on the middle piece of wood. They were used in sets of two for floating or walking on water. This must have required hours of training and incredible balance to perform. All attempts in modern times to emulate this feat have been unsuccessful.

## Takezutsu (Breathing Pipe)

When the *Ninja* was crossing water under the gaze of enemy guards or being pursued, the *Ninja* would use the *Takezutsu*. Made from a reed or piece of bamboo, similar to a snorkle, he could remain under water for long periods of time and the innocent piece of reed or bamboo sticking out of the water would not arouse suspicion.

# KAKI (Fire Tools)

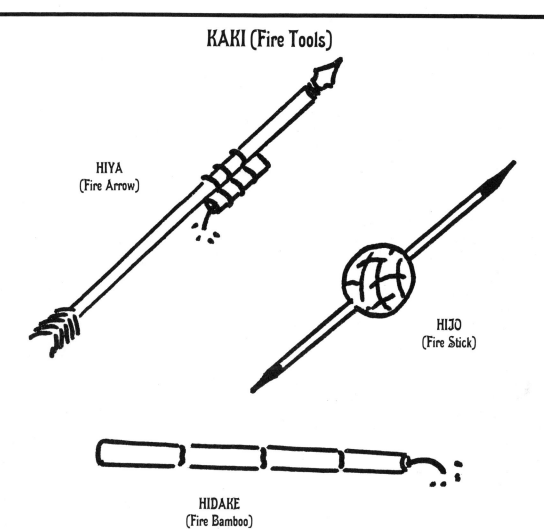

**HIYA**
(Fire Arrow)

**HIJO**
(Fire Stick)

**HIDAKE**
(Fire Bamboo)

GUNPOWDER

**HIKYU (Fire Ball)**

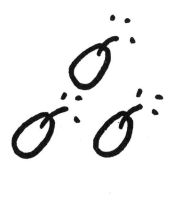

**Torinoko (Bird's Eggs)**

## Noboriki (Climbing Tools)

To be able to gather information, to reconnoitre and to kill, the *Ninja* had to get into the places and positions needed to accomplish these things, so tools for scaling walls, climbing on to roof-tops and up trees were researched and developed by the *Ninja* Groups. In a time when there were no such things as street lamps or electric light bulbs, all the methods of entering were performed in the darkness. One could easily think that the darkness made it easier for the *Ninja*, but in fact darkness brings with it a condition of silence and stillness, where any noise however small is magnified and easily heard.

The *Ninja* would always make for the highest point of a castle or dwelling, knowing that the higher he was, the harder it would be to hear any sounds.

## Tobibashigo (Throwing Ladder)
## Kagiwara (Hook Rope)

The *Ninja* used a *Tobibashigo*, which were slats of bamboo tied together in the shape of a ladder. At the top end of the two pieces of rope a large iron hook was attached. This would be thrown upwards and once the hook had been secured, the wall could be easily climbed by the *Ninja*.

The *Kagiwara* was a long piece of rope with an iron hook tied to one end. Usually a single hook was used but sometimes two or even three hooks would be tied to the end of the rope. This was used in the same way as the *Tobibashigo*.

## Shinobikagi (Secret Hook)
## Shinobitsue (Secret Stick)

Walking sticks were covered in the weapon section, but the *Ninja* also converted them into climbing tools. The *Shinobikagi* appeared to be just an ordinary walking stick, but when opened separated into five sections with a rope running through the middle of the bamboo stick. A hook at one end was used to secure the stick and the *Ninja* would place his feet on the separated sections to climb up.

The *Shinobitsue* was also a walking stick but the hook was not attached to a rope but to the end of the stick. Holes were made through the bamboo and pieces of rope were passed through the holes and tied to form a loop. The *Ninja* would place his feet in the loops and climb up or just support his weight while he looked around.

## Kasugai (Clamps)

These were used for climbing up castle walls in the same manner as they are used by mountain climbers today. However, the *Ninja* had a special way of using them when he was being pursued through a house. Remembering that infiltration was done in the darkness, should his presence be detected, he would have to hide in a place that would never be searched. Most of the hiding places were very obvious to the pursuers so the *Ninja* would lie on the ceiling. This was made possible by the *Kasugai*, which he would stick in the ceiling and by taking up a reverse press-up position would lie on the ceiling as the pursuers passed underneath. This of course requires incredible strength of the arms, but with the *Ninja's* training, a simple feat to perform.

## Kaiki (Opening Tools)

Once the *Ninja* had successfully entered the castle grounds or the garden of a dwelling, he would then have to open doors and windows to get into the living-quarters of the enemy. If he were gathering information or stealing documents, he would have to pick locks or break open boxes. For these purposed the *Ninja* carried a variety of opening tools.

## Kunai (Blade)

Shaped like a trowel and made of iron, it was used to open doors, dig in the earth and if needs be thrown like a *Shuriken*.

## Shikoro (Saw)

This was a triangular shaped saw, used like an ordinary saw to cut wood, but was also used by the *Ninja* to make holes in walls and ceilings. With its triangular shape, the hole made in the wall would leave a small opening on the inside, thereby harder to be discovered by the occupants of the room and larger on the outside, enabling him to get a clear view into the room.

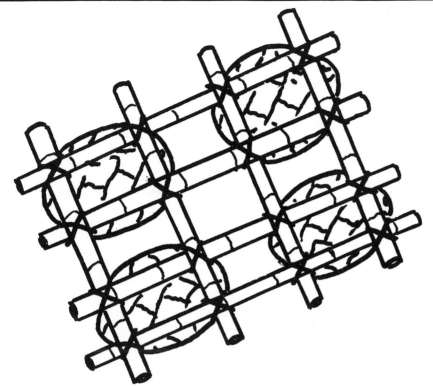

KAMEIKADA
(Tortoise Raft)

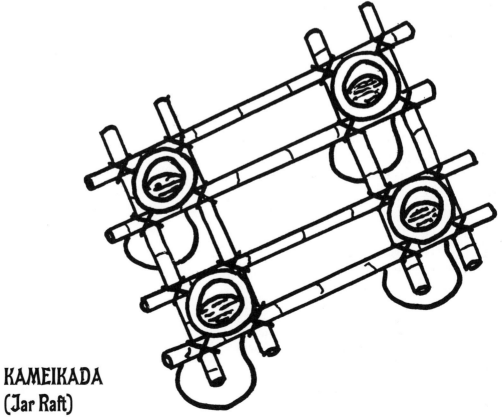

KAMEIKADA
(Jar Raft)

## Togime (Jammer) Shimeki (Closer)

At certain times it would be necessary for the *Ninja* to jam doors, such as when he was being pursued through a house and this he did by using a *Tojime* or a *Shimeki*. Remember that the doors of Japanese rooms are sliding doors; these tools were made of metal with hooks at either end.

## Tsubogiri (Opener)

This tool was made of iron and had an arc shaped piece at one end. Like a crescent moon, they came in various sizes but all had two very sharp points at the ends of the crescent. By holding the handle and slowly turning the *Tsubogiri*, the *Ninja* cut a hole in a wall, through which he passed a bamboo tube. This would make it easier for him to listen in on secret conversations and if his orders were to kill, the tube would be used as a blowpipe for his poison tipped darts.

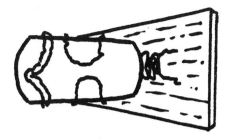

MIZUKAKIGETA (Web Sandals)

TAKEZUTSU (Bamboo Pipe)

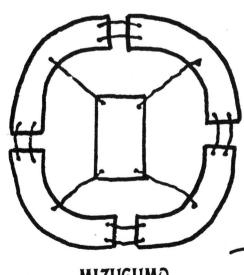

MIZUGUMO
(Water Spider)

METHOD OF CROSSING WATER

# NOBORIKI (Climbing Tools)

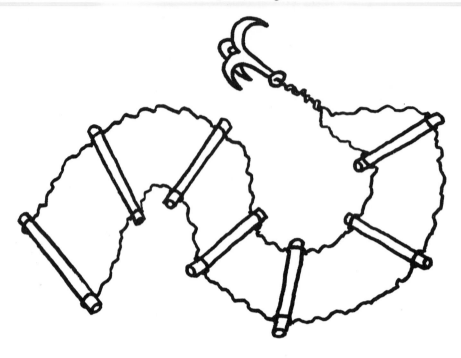

TOBIBASHIGO (Throwing Ladder)

KAGIWARA (Hook Rope)

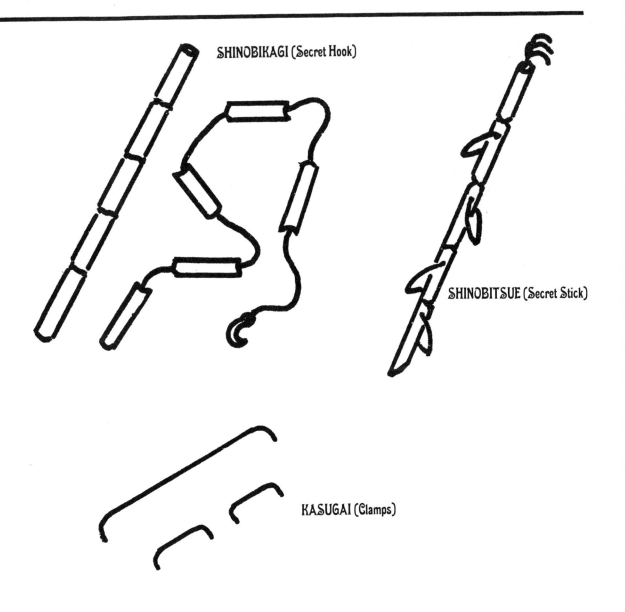

SHINOBIKAGI (Secret Hook)

SHINOBITSUE (Secret Stick)

KASUGAI (Clamps)

LYING ON CEILING

GYAKU UDETATE (Upside Down Press-Ups)

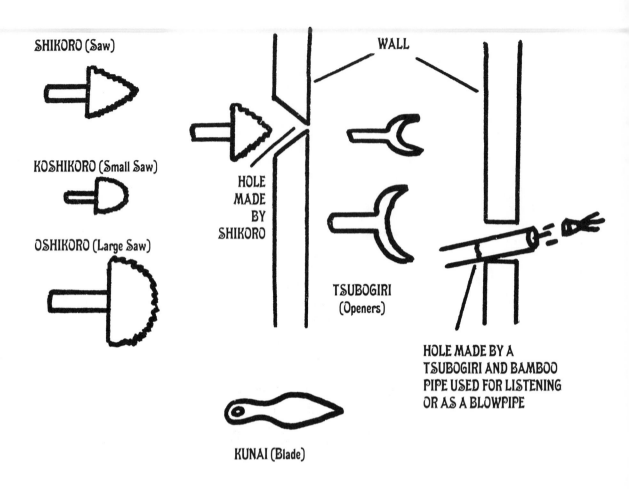

SHIKORO (Saw)

KOSHIKORO (Small Saw)

OSHIKORO (Large Saw)

WALL

HOLE MADE BY SHIKORO

TSUBOGIRI (Openers)

HOLE MADE BY A TSUBOGIRI AND BAMBOO PIPE USED FOR LISTENING OR AS A BLOWPIPE

KUNAI (Blade)

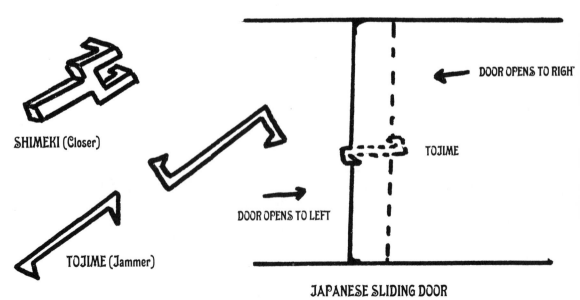

SHIMEKI (Closer)

TOJIME (Jammer)

DOOR OPENS TO RIGHT

TOJIME

DOOR OPENS TO LEFT

JAPANESE SLIDING DOOR

術

# JUTSU

## (METHOD)

# Ninjutsu 'The Method'

*Ninjutsu*, the Art or Way of the *Ninja*, was divided into two distinct Sections: *Yonin* and *Innin*.

*Yonin* was entering the enemy's territory in disguise for the purpose of gathering information, stealing secret documents and killing.

*Innin* was the *Ninja*, dressed in his dark *Shinobifuku* (Secret Outfit), climbing walls or over rooftops, hiding in the shadows for the purpose of spying and assassination.

## Yonin (Sunlight Secret)

The *Ninja*, who was a master of disguise, would infiltrate the enemy's towns and castles dressed as a priest, doctor, traveller, beggar and even a woman. It was essential that not only did he look like the different people he was playing but also to gain the confidence of the people and to allay suspicion he would have to be able to perform the work or duties of the trades. From an early age the *Ninja*, as part of his training, would study religion, medicines, dialects and customs of many areas. In disguise they could scout out an intended dwelling and having learnt the layout of the place and the number of inhabitants could then come back later at night, dressed in their *Shinobifuku* and secretly enter the place.

When disguised as a beggar, the *Ninja* would eat his own poisons to make his body weak and his face take on an emaciated appearance. Pulling out one's own teeth was also done to add to the effect of being a beggar.

The *Ninja* would also put the scales of fishes in their eyes to give the impression that they were blind.

Preparing for the future or for any unforeseen circumstances was one of the most important teachings of *Ninjutsu*, so when a *Ninja* travelled about the country, as they passed houses, walls and dwellings, they would drop seeds in the ground and these seeds would grow into trees to be used by the *Ninja* many years later.

## Tabidatsu (Setting out on a Journey)

Once a *Ninja* had received his orders, he would leave the valley, where he had lived and trained and set off on the long journey that would take him to the place where he would fulfil his mission. In a time when there were no maps as such and none of the modern equipment available to travellers nowadays, the *Ninja* only had himself and Nature to rely on. Problems such as time, direction, distance, communication, weather, food and water all had to be overcome and these problems were dealt with in the Art of *Ninjutsu*.

There was only one way to travel and that was on foot, so the *Ninja* would start running, covering over one hundred kilometres a day over very difficult terrain. In his clothing he had special pockets enabling him to go to the toilet while running without taking off his clothes and stopping. They also learnt to eat, drink and sleep while they were running.

While travelling it was important to measure distances and these measurements were left by secret markings on rocks and trees to be used by other members of the Group. To measure distances the *Ninja* learnt to run, placing one foot directly infront of the other and counting the steps as he ran along.

To communicate the *Ninja* used a system of coloured grains of rice to pass messages. Using the five colours; red, yellow, black, blue and white and by mixing the colours in set combinations, the *Ninja* placed the grains of rice at the sides of roads, under stones, in bird's nests and in the hollows of trees. The grains of rice were first baked hard before being dyed so as not to be eaten by hungry birds or animals.

When disguised as musicians, the *Ninja* also communicated with each other by using flutes and *Shamisen* (Japanese Banjo). The tunes or arrangements of notes spelt out different kinds of coded messages. These arrangements consisted of a forty-eight note series similar to Morse Code.

## Kishaku (Magnet)

To judge direction the *Ninja* read the position of stars and also used a *Kishaku*. This was a piece of metal about five centimetres long and two centimetres thick, which was placed on a leaf. The leaf was then placed on water and the *Kishaku* would spin around and point to the North. The knowledge of the Compass was known by the *Ninja* years before the Portuguese Ships brought the traders from Europe to Japan.

Nourishment was another problem, as the *Ninja* would never know how long it would take to complete a mission. For obvious reasons he could not

# GANDO (Eye Light)

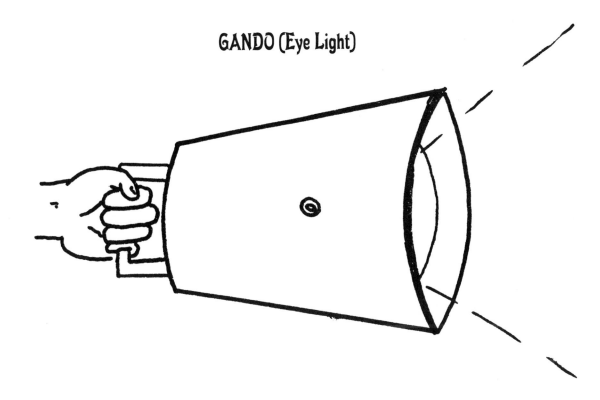

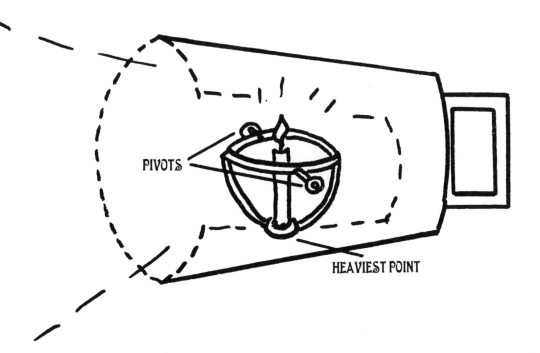

PIVOTS

HEAVIEST POINT

carry lots of provisions so the *Ninja* had to get his food and water along the way. In the open this was an easy thing for him to do, being a trained herbalist he knew which flowers and plants to eat. Butterbur, osmond, dogtooth violet, bracken, shepherd's purse, mountain lily, parsley and chickenweed were some of the plants used by the *Ninja* as food.

When travelling through the mountains or in the hot season, the *Ninja* employed five methods for finding water.

1) He would stick the feather of a bird in the ground and wait. If after several hours the feather was wet, he knew there was water nearby.

2) He would dig a hole in the earth down to about three feet and by placing his ear to the ground, he could hear or feel the movement of water under the earth.

3) If he found ant's nests or large numbers of crickets in a certain area, he would know that water was nearby.

4) He recognised plants and flowers that only grew in areas near to water.

5) By looking across at the shapes of hills and valleys he could tell by the formation of the landscape where the rivers and lakes would be.

To make the deadly poisons for the *Shuriken*, the *Fukiya* (Blow Darts) and the *Fukibari* (Spitting Needles) the *Ninja* usually used the Aconite seed. However the Jimson weed, the blowfish and certain insect eggs were also used to make poisons. Thorns from nettles were used to make itching powder and sweat from a toad was mixed into a potion and when drunk made a person numb.

Once a *Ninja* reached populated areas, he would only travel by night and certainly all his infiltrations of castles and dwellings were made under cover of darkness. However, darkness brought with it hazards for the *Ninja*, such as losing his way, running into people unexpectedly and the fact that he was travelling at night was suspicious, which was something a *Ninja* always tried to avoid.

To see in the darkness, the *Ninja* would lie on the ground and look up at the night sky. Then, when he looked into the darkness it made it possible for him to see more clearly.

When the *Ninja* was travelling through the darkness, if he saw the lights from lanterns or candles coming towards him, it was very important for him to know how far away they were. This he did by holding his hand in front of his face with the fingers stretched out horizontally. The lights that he could see above his outstretched fingers were further away than the lights below his fingers.

# Gando (Eyelight)

Sometimes at night, the *Ninja* carried a *Gando*. This was a kind of torch made of a piece of flat metal bent into a tube shape with a candle inside. Whichever way the *Gando* was pointed; up, forward or down, the candle always remained in an upright position. This was made possible by the use of weights and pivot rods.

Travelling through long reeds or grass was always very dangerous as the movement might be seen by the enemy, so the *Ninja* would wait for the wind to rise and move the grass before making his way through it. As noise made by the dry reeds or grass would certainly alert the enemy guards, the *Ninja* would wait till after it had rained before approaching an enemy camp.

When a *Ninja* was escaping or being pursued by the enemy, he would run into the wind. He had been trained to keep his eyes open, even in the strongest gales and so could make his escape while the pursuers would be hampered by the wind blowing in their faces. Similarly, bright sunshine was used in the same manner. The *Ninja* being able to keep his eyes open in direct sunlight, whereas the pursuers would have to shade their eyes. Having practiced running over all kinds of terrain and under any conditions, the *Ninja* could easily outdistance his pursuers when it was raining, as the enemy would be sliding about and falling, unable to make progress on wet slippery surfaces.

As there were no calenders or watches, to tell the time, the day and the month, the *Ninja* used the length of shadows to tell the time and the positions of the sun and moon to know what day or month it was when he travelled.

# Nekome (Cat's Eyes)

The *Ninja* also used a method called *Nekome* to tell the time. By looking at the pupils of a cat's eyes he knew what time it was by the shape of the pupils. 6 a.m. was a Ball shape: 8 a.m. was the shape of an Egg: 10 a.m. was the shape of a seed: midday was the shape of a needle: 2 p.m. was a seed shape: 4 p.m. was an egg shape: 6 p.m. was the shape of a ball.

The *Ninja* knew of the body-clock and learnt to regulate his natural functions. By controlling his bodily functions to only operate at certain times during the day, during his training, when the *Ninja* was on a mission he used these feelings to tell the time.

NEKOME (Cat's Eyes)

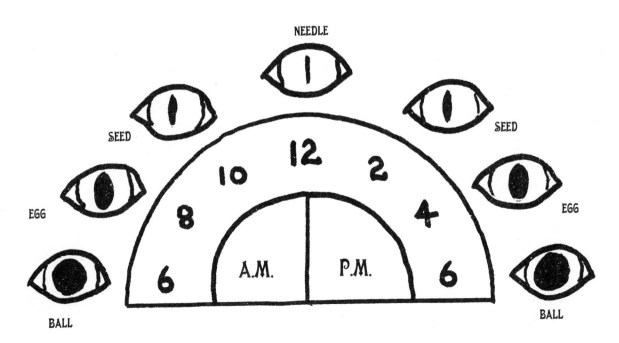

# ONGYO
## (Hiding Forms)

HIDING BEHIND ROCKS

ESCAPING BY USE OF KAYAKU (Fire Powder)

HIDING IN REEDS

HIDING IN TREES

HIDING IN ROOFS

## Innin (Shadow Secret)

## 'Make the Night your Friend and the Darkness your Cloak of Invisibility'.

Perhaps the most difficult part of a *Ninja's* work was getting into a place, completing the mission and getting out again without the enemy knowing that he had been there. This was absolutely vital in cases of gathering information and spying. If the enemy discovered that their plans or conversations were known to the opposing forces, they could easily change them, thereby making the *Ninja's* efforts worthless.

Having travelled from his valley and safely arrived at the castle or dwelling which was to be infiltrated, the *Ninja* would then set about the difficult task of getting into the place. Large dwellings were easier to enter, as the responsibility for guarding the place was divided among many people, most unacquainted with each other, thereby making it that much less difficult for the *Ninja* to secretly enter and go about his dangerous work.

The most difficult dwelling would be the single large house, occupied by an official, a Lord or perhaps a senior officer in the enemy's army. These were the major targets and to this end the *Ninja* applied the Art of *Innin*.

One of the greatest hazards facing a *Ninja* was the dog. Most dwellings at that time used watchdogs to guard the premises, so this problem had to be dealt with by the *Ninja*. Once the *Ninja* had entered the dwelling, he did not know how long he would have to remain hidden, waiting for the right opportunity to gather the information he needed or to kill the person he had been sent to assassinate. Because of this, just killing the dog would only arouse suspicion and the people of the house would know at once that they had been infiltrated by a *Ninja* and set about finding him.

The *Ninja* would first visit the dwelling by day, disguised as a priest or a beggar, to establish if there were a dog guarding the house. If there were, he would then decide on a method to deal with the dog from the many that were part of *Innin*.

Usually male dogs were used to guard houses, so the *Ninja* would bring a female dog on heat to keep the watchdog occupied while he made his entry. Being experts in animal and bird mimicry, if the dog barked, the *Ninja* would bark back at the dog and the people in the dwelling would think it was just the noise of a dog fight. Other methods included food filled with poisons or metal shavings that would slowly kill the dog. The *Ninja* would wait as the dog gradually became sick and died. The owner would then have to get another dog and in the period when there was no watchdog, the *Ninja* would make his entry. Sleeping powders and potions to cause numbness were known and used by the *Ninja*.

Other methods of gaining entry to a dwelling were used, such as causing diversions. The *Ninja* would set fire to houses nearby and in the ensuing panic quickly enter the house.

In the Art of *Ninjutsu*, there are recorded the Eight Best Times for entering a dwelling.

1) The Night when a sick person finally recovers from an illness.

2) The Night when heavy drinking has taken place.

3) The Night when a fire has broken out at a nearby dwelling.

4) The Night when a celebration has taken place for the refurnishing of a house.

5) The Night when someone has died in the house.

6) The Night when there is a storm or heavy rain.

7) The Night when a commotion has taken place, such as a brawl or a visit from an official.

8) The Wedding Night.

Once the *Ninja* has successfully entered the dwelling, he would make his way to the main living rooms. He would climb up into the roof part of the house or attic and conceal himself above the ceiling of the main room. From there he would eavesdrop on the conversations of the people in the house and depending on his mission, whether it was to gather information or to kill, the *Ninja* would learn the routine of the household.

To begin with he would do nothing but wait. He would remain perfectly still, knowing that any sound he made would alert the inhabitants to his presence and the mission would fail or he would be killed. This waiting could be days or even weeks and in all that time he would have to endure hours upon hours of remaining motionless controlling his breathing and going without food or water.

# IN O MUSUBI
## (Making the Sign)

**FUGENSANMAIYA**
(All Wisdom is Devotion)

**DAIKONGORIN**
(Large Gold Ring)

**GEJISHI**
(Outer Lion)

**NAIJISHI**
(Inner Lion)

**GEIBAKU**
(Outer Bond)

**NAIBAKU**
(Inner Bond)

**CHIKEN**
(Bond of Wisdom)

**NICHIRIN**
(Circle of the Sun)

**ONGYO**
(Hidden Forms)

The problem of food was not that worrying to the *Ninja*, as they always carried small tablets or pills, which were made from honey, grains of wheat, carrot, rice and sake wine. These vitamin pills were eaten three times a day and in this way it was possible for him to survive for about ten days to two weeks.

A much greater problem was that of water but the *Ninja* overcame this using several methods. First the obvious one, of when the inhabitants of the house were asleep, he would take a drink of water from the kitchen. Taking a drink of water would go unnoticed, but if he helped himself to food, the loss would easily be discovered. Secondly, to stop himself from feeling thirsty or his throat from becoming dry for want of liquid, the *Ninja* would suck sesame seeds or chew leeks. The sap from the leeks was also placed on the inside of the nostrils and this would take away the feeling of thirst. The sap of the leeks would also keep him warm in winter. Lastly in his training of *Mudo* (Stillness) he had practiced going without food and water for long periods of time.

## Benjo (Toilet)

The *Ninja*, as stated earlier, had special pockets in his clothing to use when he wanted to go to the toilet. Usually the *Ninja* would empty his bowels before he entered a dwelling and as he would then only exist on his tablets and sesame seeds the problem of bowel movement would not occur for some time.

However the *Ninja* did visit the toilet in the house, not to use it but to gather information about the people of the house and their routine. The Japanese toilet is a large hole in the ground, usually twenty inches long and about twelve inches wide. Below the hole was a deep pit where all the matter accumulated. By examining the excrement, the *Ninja* could learn how many people lived in the house, if they were sick or healthy, what time they got up in the mornings, went to bed at night and even mealtimes. A wealth of information could be gathered from these pits and once a *Ninja* hid for days in the pit and assassinated a Lord when he came to relieve himself.

After having learnt the routine of the house, the *Ninja* would choose an appropriate time to get his information or kill the person. He would then, as secretly as he had entered the house, escape and make his way back to his Group.

"The Invisible Men". "The Invisible Assassins". "The Men with no Shadow". "The Disappearing Ones".

These were some of the names by which the *Ninja* was known and they came about by the *Ninja's* ability to melt into his surroundings, to vanish into thin air and to appear out of nowhere. The tricks or techniques employed to create these effects, if looked at now are all only diversionary tactics, distracting the enemy's attention, but to the people at that time they were astonishing and terrifying.

## Ongyo (Hiding Forms)

If the enemy approached, the *Ninja* would quickly hide behind a rock or climb up a tree. He covered his mouth with his sleeve and would remain perfectly still for hours. He would dig a hole in the earth and hide in it or by using a *Takezutsu* (Bamboo Pipe), he could remain under water as his pursuers passed by the river not noticing the innocent looking reed sticking out of the water. Sometimes when he was hiding he would imitate the sound of a bird or an animal and at other times, he would throw a pebble into the bushes on the opposite side to where he was hiding. When the enemy went to investigate the noise he would make his escape.

If the *Ninja* was surrounded by the enemy he would use *Kayaku* (Fire Powder) which would explode, giving out a dense smoke and using the surprise and confusion caused by the smoke, the *Ninja* would make his escape. This tactic was also used when attacking the enemy.

From these methods of escape and attack came the legend of the Invisible Assassins.

## In O Musubi (Making the Sign)
## Kettsuin (Mixing Signs)

The method called *In O Musubi* was believed to make the *Ninja* invisible and to give him supernatural powers and even immortality. Before a *Ninja* went into an attack or while hiding behind rocks or trees, the *Ninja* would perform *Kettsuin* with his fingers. He believed that it would make him immune from harm and give him strength.

This is similar to Christians, who make the sign of the Cross for protection against evil or before doing something dangerous.

The number 9 has always been associated with Magic by the Priests and Holy Men of the Orient, because any number (from 1 to 9) multiplied by nine becomes nine: $9 \times 5 = 45$ $(4 + 5 = 9)$.

This pattern of signs was made up of Nine Lines: Five horizontal and Four vertical. The horizontal lines were the odd numbers: 1, 3, 5, 7, 9 and the vertical lines were the even numbers: 2, 4, 6, 8. Each line was given a Character and a meaning.

**Horizontal Lines.** 1 — *Rin* (Comfort) 3 — *Toh* (Fight) 5 — *Kai* (All) 7 — *Retsu* (Tear) 9 — *Zen* (Before)

**Vertical Lines.** 2 — *Hei* (Soldier) 4 — *Sha* (Man) 6 — *Jin* (Battle) 8 — *Zai* (Is, To Be)

By cutting the air in front of himself, vertically and horizontally, with his right hand the *Ninja* would cast a spell to protect himself.

The Second method of *In O Musibi* and *Kettsuin* which the *Ninja* believed would make him invisible and give him supernatural powers was finger combination of Nine different shapes. The Ninja performed these shapes with his fingers as he waited in the roof of a dwelling or when hiding in trees.

These Nine finger formations were also given Japanese Characters and meanings.
1) *Fugensanmaiya* (All Wisdom is Devotion)
2) *Daikongorin* (Large Gold Ring)
3) *Gejishi* (Outer Lion)
4) *Naijishi* (Inner Lion)
5) *Geibaku* (Outer Bond)
6) *Naibaku* (Inner Bond)
7) *Chiken* (Bond of Wisdom)
8) *Nichirin* (Circle of the Sun)
9) *Ongyo* (Hidden Forms)

What in fact the *Ninja* was doing with *In O Musubi* and *Kettsuin* was a from of meditation to relax himself in preparation for the coming ordeal or to endure the suffering he was going through. Many Oriental Mystics place great emphasis on the parts of the hands and fingers.

They believe that every part of the hand relates directly to the vital organs of the body and by rubbing or massaging the hands a soothing or curing effect can be transmitted to different parts of the body. If and when a *Ninja* was nervous, he would grab the base of the third finger on the left hand with the fingers of the right hand. By squeezing hard, a relaxing and pleasant feeling would fill his body and the nervous tension would disappear.

The fear of death was not a fear that the *Ninja* carried with him, but failure to complete a mission was the greatest fear that the *Ninja* lived with. They sometimes worked in twoes and one would give his life so that the other one could complete the mission. For example, two *Ninjas* would enter a dwelling and one of them would allow himself to be captured and killed. This would put the inhabitants of the house at ease and make it easier for the second *Ninja* to gather the necessary information.

If a mission was to assassinate a Lord, once again the first *Ninja* would allow himself to be caught, thereby putting the intended victim off guard and the second *Ninja* would make the killing.

## Keika (Firefly)

One of the *Ninja's* major functions was to carry documents, and messages and this was very dangerous work, for should he be captured, he would most certainly be tortured and made to give information about his mission. The *Ninja* used a method called *Keika*, which involved a very intricate game of bluff and double-bluff.

Whenever a *Ninja* was caught carrying documents or messages, the captors would never know for certain if they were true or false. Thus began the game of bluff and double-bluff. Unable to bear the torture any longer the *Ninja* would confess (?). If he were carrying true information, he would say it was false and confess the true message, which was false. Are you with me so far? This contingency would always be taken care of, because a second *Ninja* carrying the false information, that is the information that the tortured *Ninja* said was true, would purposely get himself captured and as his information would be the same as the information given under torture by the first *Ninja*, the enemy would believe it was true. Needless to say that both *Ninjas* would kill themselves or be killed.

It was also common practice to send false information, which was intended to fall into the hands of the enemy and the *Ninja* would be hired to perform this work knowing beforehand that he was going to his death. Once again the method of *Keika* would be used. The *Ninja* caught with the false information would stick to this story enduring all kinds of torture and a second *Ninja* would be captured and the false information confirmed and believed by the enemy.

## KUNOICHI (Female Ninja)

Japanese
Character 'KU'

Japanese
Character 'NO'

Japanese
Character 'ICHI'

Japanese Character 'ONNA' (Woman)

## Kunoichi (Ninja Woman)

Within all *Ninja* Groups was a method known as *Kunoichi*. In Japanese Characters, the symbol for *Ku*, *No*, *Ichi*, when put together forms the word *Onna*, the symbol for Woman.

This method consisted of two parts. The first would involve the *Ninja* disguising himself as a woman to infiltrate dwellings or castles. However, this disguise could only be used for a short time as in Japanese Society, the custom of taking a bath every day and all together, men and women, meant that the *Ninja* would soon be uncovered.

The second method was to use female *Ninjas*. The training and the techniques they learnt were almost the same as their male counterparts, though they did not wear the *Shinobifuku* (Secret Outfit) and creep about over rooftops at night. Their effectiveness was in the method of *Yonin* (Sunlight Secret).

As a young girl, she would enter the enemy's castles and work as a maid, servant or shop person. Over the years, as they grew up, they would become totally accepted in these roles and then at a later date be called upon to gather information or to help a *Ninja* to secretly enter the castle. These women would often marry and bear children by men in the Lord's employ, carefully selected by the *Jonin* (High Rank) of their *Ninja* Groups.

There were some instances where the female *Ninja* would fall in love with their husbands and knew that the information they passed on might result in the death of the man she loved. Torn between these two emotions of love for their husbands and duty to their Groups, it would be a very painful decision as to which course to take. However, duty to her Group would win out, for should she not pass on information she was expeced to know or gave false information, a *Ninja* would be sent to kill her.

This period in Japanese History, when the *Ninja* was used, extended over hundreds of years and rivalry and wars between the Great Warlords continued from one generation to another so the method of *Netane* (Sleeping Seed), which meant putting a young *Ninja* into the enemy camp and not calling on their services until many years later, was an important and well used method in the Art of *Ninjutsu*.

## Yashiki (House)

A *Ninja's Yashiki* was a maze of secret doors, passageways, walls and stairways. Seen from the outside it appeared to have only one floor, in fact they contained two or even sometimes three floors. These floors were built with different ceiling heights and were only accessible through secret doors and stairways.

False passageways that led nowhere, walls that opened and led to secret rooms and doors that didn't open, all built to confuse an intruder. The floors were made with different levels so that if a rival *Ninja* had infiltrated the house in the dark, he would trip up and give himself away. When a *Ninja* was being chased by the enemy, he would run along a corridor that led to a stairway leading down. The *Ninja* would quickly conceal himself behind a secret door and the enemy, thinking that the *Ninja* had gone down the steps would follow, but would realise too late that the steps in fact suddenly stopped and the enemy would fall down into a pit with bamboo spikes sticking out at the bottom and he would be impaled.

*Ninja* groups were sometimes the targets for other *Ninja* Groups, so each house had its own unique variations of secret walls and passageways.

In *Shiga* Prefecture in Japan, a *Ninja Yashiki* of the *Koga* Group can still be seen to this day.

# I AM NINJA: MY WAY IS NINJITSU

# 話
## WA
## (STORY)

# The Method of Netane (Sleeping Seed)

The last snows of winter had begun to melt and the warm winds from the south blew over the silent valley in Shiga Prefecture, Japan. The white colour of the snow-covered mountains had changed to brown and the valley, which was the home of the Koga Ninja Group, took on a lush green as spring once more came to warm the houses and training halls of the Ninja.

For Junko, a young girl with large brown eyes and long straight jet-black hair that almost reached down to her waist, it was a time of sadness and joy. She had been born in th valley and after twelve years of severe training she was to begin a mission that would take her hundred of miles away from her home and family.

Japan had entered the Sengoku Era, the Age of Wars, and the country had been plunged into a nation of chaos as Great Lords made wars, each trying to extend his boundaries, build up his armies and dreamed of uniting Japan under one ruler, the Shogun.

All the Ninja Groups were kept busy and these times of strife would become known as the Golden Age of the Ninja.

The young twelve year old girl, the daughter of a Chunin Ninja (Middle Rank) from one of the fifty-three families that made up the Koga Ninja Group, accompanied by an older woman set off for the Castle town of the Great Warlord Tagawa.

The two women, after a journey of three weeks, finally reached the Castle town and the young Junko was placed in the store of a half-caste grain merchant. The Master was half Chinese and half Japanese and the grain from his store was used to make a kind of bread eaten at the tables of the soldiers that lived inside the Castle.

The young girl's duties were to sweep and clean the house of her Master and to sew the cloth bags that carried the grain. She slept in the grain store on the bags that she sewed and getting up at daybreak, working till dusk and sleeping would be her life for the next two and half years.

In the autumn of 1568, she received a message from her Ninja group, telling her to get a certain young man, who worked in the Tax office of the Great Lord Tagawa, to notice her. The young man, who was called Taro, was the assistant to the 3rd assistant to the Tax Collector and had recently arrived from the northern part of Japan. He looked a likely prospect for promotion and advancement in the service of the Great Lord Tagawa and it would be a good opportunity for her to enter the inner walls of the Castle if she were to marry him.

When she heard that a band of entertainers and musicians was visiting the town, the young girl, now fourteen and a half, arranged to accidently meet the man she had been ordered to marry. She went with her Master to the square where the entertainers were performing and in the midst of a group of young men, laughing and drinking, the Master pointed out the young man Taro to her.

He was a boy of sixteen, with a serious but gentle appearance and the young girl was glad that such a pleasant boy had been chosen for her. By accidently bumping into him among the boisterous crowd of revellers, it was an easy and natural situation that brought about their first meeting. After the initial apologies, their eyes met and she quickly looked away with just enough feeling of embarrassment and shyness, that would make the boy look after her as she walked away down the street, accompanied by her Master.

During the next year, two or three more accidental meetings were enough for the boy to decide that the girl who worked in the grain store would make a good wife for him and she looked strong enough to bear him healthy sons.

The young Taro told the official who worked above him in the Tax office of his intentions, and after money was exchanged, the young girl from the grain store moved into his small quarters in the Tax building, as his wife.

Five years passed and now the boy Taro had been promoted to the treasury office of the Great Lord Tagawa and his household, including his wife and son, aged four, were moved inside the castle walls. He had been noticed by the Chief Official of the Great Lord Tagawa and his hard work and the serious way he conducted his responsibilities was gaining him access to areas of the castle, that would prove useful to the Ninjas at a later date.

In the winter of Tenjo 2 (1574), Junko received a message telling her to gather information on the layout of the sewer system that led out of the Castle into the river below the Castle walls. This information was passed back to her Group and on one dark night, while her husband and young son was fast asleep, she made her way to the sewer outlet and kept lookout as a Ninja, wearing the dark cloth of the Shinobifuku (Secret Outfit) climbed up the

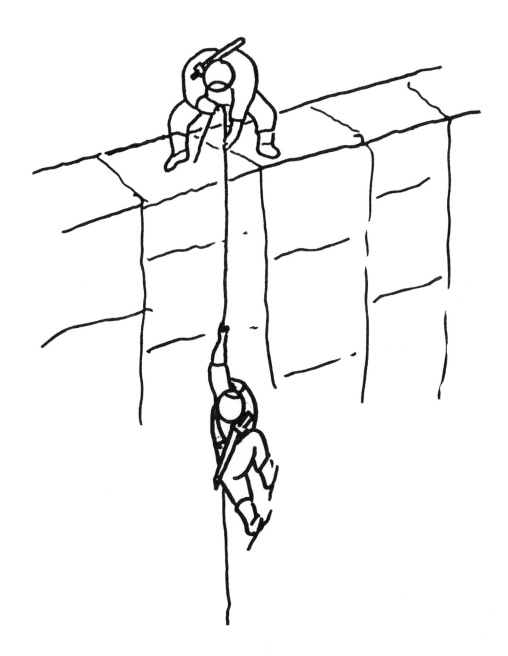

castle wall and made his way into the inner part of the Castle. For the next five nights, she crept out of her house in the darkness and waited by the sewer outlet. On the fifth night, the Ninja re-appeared and she helped him climb out through the sewer outlet and scale down the castle wall. She silently watched as he disappeared into the night, knowing that he was returning to the green valley that had once been her home and wondered if she would ever see her family again.

In the year Tenjo 6 (1578), she had heard that the Great Lord of Japan, Oda Nobunaga, who was said to have gone crazy with drink had sent an army against the Iga Ninja Group and had destroyed the crops and houses in the valley in Mie Prefecture. When the troops had arrived the Ninjas had gone and a hatred of the Ninja had brought on severe reprisals against anyone who was suspected of being a Ninja.

As she poured out the tea for her husband, now a highly respected revenue officer in the employ of the Great Lord Tagawa, and looked across at her ten year old son playing with a toy wooden sword in the garden, she felt that the world outside of suspicion, intrigue and death was not part of the tranquil world she now lived in with her new family.

This peace and contentment was suddenly shattered, when her husband began to work late every night for about two weeks. He did not inform her as to the reason why he had been working very hard recently, but this was normal in the society of Japan at that time. The wife's duties were only concerned with the home and looking after the children and did not concern itself with the business of the husband. However, one night her husband returned late and he had been drinking heavily and seemed to be very angry. He began to complain about the hard work that he had been forced to do, because the Great Lord Tagawa was planning to send five thousand troops to the eastern region as an auxiliary force to join up the Oda Nobunaga's armies. All the money and the paper work had to be finished quickly, as the soldiers were to begin their march at the end of the month and he would have to go with the soldiers as assistant pay master.

After her husband had passed out and lay beside her in a drunken stupor, she lay awake knowing that the information she had been told by her husband was of vital importance and that she would have to get that information back to her Group. Tears filled her eyes as she looked across at the man she had grown to love and knew that that information she would give to the Ninjas would result in an ambush of the five thousand troops and the massacre that would follow would leave most, if not all dead at the hands of the Ninjas.

The following day, when she went shopping in the town, she called in at the grain store that had been her home for two and a half years, and in the back room met the woman, who had twelve years ago travelled with her on the long journey from the valley in Shiga Prefecture to the Castle of the Great Lord Tagawa. After telling the woman about the five thousand soldiers leaving at the end of the month for the eastern region, she left the store to buy vegetables she needed for her husband's dinner that night.

At the end of the month, as she hung out the washing behind her house in the inner castle, she noticed that everything appeared normal. There was no excited activity, such as the cleaning of armour or the sharpening of weapons, gathering of equipment or stores that would always precede a large group of soldiers, that were preparing to go on a march. Perhaps all the preparations were being done in secret and as quietly as possible, not to arouse suspicion in the town. That must be it she thought as she carried the now empty washing basket into the house. Her husband still continued to work late every night and had not confided in her a second time as to the reason why he was working so hard.

The end of the month had passed and the beginning of a new month had come. The life in the Castle had remained the same but for the last few days her husband had not returned to the house. As she lay in bed alone, unable to sleep, she began to feel that something was terribly wrong and decided that the following day she would go to the grain store and find out what happened and even perhaps get help for her family to flee the Castle. With these thoughts in her mind she fell asleep and just as dawn was breaking, she was woken by the sound of soldiers bursting into her house. The soldiers took her arms and began to drag her away. Her young twelve year old son attacked the soldiers with his wooden sword, to stop them hurting his mother and one of the soldiers with a single cut with the blade of his sword, severed the boy's head from his shoulders and it rolled into a corner of the room like an unwanted ball.

After three days of torture, where she had been abused by dozens of soldiers, her hands and her feet had been crushed but she had said nothing.

She had not revealed that she was a Ninja. On the fourth day she was taken to a large room inside the Castle and thrown down on the floor, her arms and legs tied with ropes. She could hear voices and tried to open her eyes to see where she was, but as her torurers had burnt her eye-lids with red hot irons, she found it too painful.

As she lay there, listening to the two men who were talking, she realised that one of the voices belonged to her husband and she heard that the information that he had given her had been a plan to entrap her. The story of the five thousand troops leaving for the eastern region at the end of the month had all been lies and she heard her husband laugh, when the other voice told him that they had sent spies to the region and had discovered hundreds of Ninjas hiding in the surrounding forests waiting for the soldiers that would never arrive.

That night she was garroted. A knotted rope was placed around her throat and two strong hands had pulled the rope tight and she had died. Her mangled body was thrown out through the sewer outlet that led to the river below the Castle walls.

In Tenjo 9 (1581) Oda Nobunaga sent fifty thousand soldiers into the valley of the Iga Ninjas, to wipe these killers and spies from the face of the earth. Overwhelmed by sheer numbers, the Ninjas ran away and disappeared all over Japan.

In Tenjo 10 (1582), a meeting took place in Kyoto, which was the capital of Japan at that time. Lord Tagawa and his trusted officials together with other Great Lords went to the meeting with Oda Nobunaga. After years of petty strife and wars, at last Japan seemed to be heading towards a united land under one ruler. Nobunaga and his rival Tokugawa Ieyasu, later to become the greatest Shogun in Japanese history, were two men who might be able to unite Japan.

On the second of June, 1582, Oda Nobunaga was assassinated by a person or persons unknown and all the Lords hurriedly returned to their Castles. In the chaos that followed, when the Great Lord Tagawa returned to his castle it was discovered that one of his officials was missing.

Far away in a peaceful valley, a Ninja returned home having successfullly completed a mission. A mission that had started fourteen years ago when, using the method used as Netane (Sleeping Seed), he had left the valley in the disguise of an assistant to the third, assistant to the Tax Collector of the Great Warlord Tagawa.